About Island Press

Since 1984, the nonprofit Island Press has been stimulating, shaping, and communicating the ideas that are essential for solving environmental problems worldwide. With more than 800 titles in print and some 40 new releases each year, we are the nation's leading publisher on environmental issues. We identify innovative thinkers and emerging trends in the environmental field. We work with world-renowned experts and authors to develop cross-disciplinary solutions to environmental challenges.

Island Press designs and implements coordinated book publication campaigns in order to communicate our critical messages in print, in person, and online using the latest technologies, programs, and the media. Our goal: to reach targeted audiences—scientists, policymakers, environmental advocates, the media, and concerned citizens—who can and will take action to protect the plants and animals that enrich our world, the ecosystems we need to survive, the water we drink, and the air we breathe.

Island Press gratefully acknowledges the support of its work by the Agua Fund, Inc., The Margaret A. Cargill Foundation, Betsy and Jesse Fink Foundation, The William and Flora Hewlett Foundation, The Kresge Foundation, The Forrest and Frances Lattner Foundation, The Andrew W. Mellon Foundation, The Curtis and Edith Munson Foundation, The Overbrook Foundation, The David and Lucile Packard Foundation, The Summit Foundation, Trust for Architectural Easements, The Winslow Foundation, and other generous donors.

The opinions expressed in this book are those of the author(s) and do not necessarily reflect the views of our donors.

LIFE BETWEEN BUILDINGS
Jan Gehl

Jan Gehl

LIFE BETWEEN BUILDINGS

Using Public Space

Translated by Jo Koch

Washington | Covelo | London

Note from Publisher: The original page numbering of this book has been retained to avoid confusion with the numerous existing citations of the work. Therefore standard Island Press front matter and back matter pages do not appear in this volume.

ISLAND PRESS is a trademark of the Center for Resource Economics.

Library of Congress Cataloging-in-Publication Data

Gehl, Jan, 1936-
  [Livet mellem husene. English]
  Life between buildings : using public space / Jan Gehl ; translated by Jo Koch.
    p. cm.
  Includes bibliographical references and index.
  ISBN-13: 978-1-59726-827-1 (pbk. : alk. paper)
  ISBN-10: 1-59726-827-5 (pbk. : alk. paper)
  1. City planning--Environmental aspects. 2. Public spaces.
  3. Pedestrian facilities design. 4. Open spaces. 5. Architecture and society. I. Title.
  HT166.G4413 2011
  711'.55--dc22
                        2010042702

Printed on recycled, acid-free paper ✿

Manufactured in the United States of America
    9

Keywords: city planning, urban planning, architecture, urban design, site planning, public space, city scale, traffic, pedestrian mall, plaza, street, outdoor space, bicycle path

Contents

Foreword

The first version of this book was published back in the 1970's, with the purpose of pointing out the shortcomings of the functionalistic architecture and city planning that dominated the period. The book asked for concern for the people who were to move about in the spaces between the buildings, it urged for an understanding for the subtle qualities, which throughout the history of human settlements, had been related to the meetings of people in the public spaces, and it pointed to the life between buildings as a dimension of architecture, urban design and city planning to be carefully treated.

Now some 35 years have gone by, and many architectural styles and ideologies have passed by over the years. These intervening years have also shown that careful work with the livability of cities and residential areas continues to be an important issue. The growing intensity, with which high quality public spaces are currently used around the world, as well as the increased general interest in the quality of cities and their public spaces, emphasizes this point. The character of the life between buildings changes with changes in the society situation, but the essential principles and quality criteria to be used when working for human quality in the public realm have proven to be remarkably constant.

Over the years, this book has been updated, revised, and translated into 15 languages. This, the sixth English language version bears little resemblance with the early versions. New material and new illustrations have been added, yet there has been no reason at all to change the original message which continues to be of essential importance: Take good care of the people and the precious life between the buildings.

At this time in history when cities all over the world are undergoing great changes in the process of growth and modernization, it is my hope that the humanistic planning principles presented in this book can serve as an inspiration for these important processes.

Copenhagen January 2006

Jan Gehl

1. LIFE BETWEEN BUILDINGS

Three Types of Outdoor Activities

a street scene

An ordinary day on an ordinary street. Pedestrians pass on the sidewalks, children play near front doors, people sit on benches and steps, the postman makes his rounds with the mail, two passersby greet on the sidewalk, two mechanics repair a car, groups engage in conversation. This mix of outdoor activities is influenced by a number of conditions. Physical environment is one of the factors: a factor that influences the activities to a varying degree and in many different ways. Outdoor activities, and a number of the physical conditions that influence them, are the subject of this book.

three types of outdoor activities

Greatly simplified, outdoor activities in public spaces can be divided into three categories, each of which places very different demands on the physical environment: *necessary activities, optional activities*, and *social activities*.

necessary activities
– under all conditions

Necessary activities include those that are more or less compulsory – going to school or to work, shopping, waiting for a bus or a person, running errands, distributing mail – in other words, all activities in which those involved are to a greater or lesser degree required to participate.

In general, everyday tasks and pastimes belong to this group. Among other activities, this group includes the great majority of those related to walking.

Because the activities in this group are necessary, their incidence is influenced only slightly by the physical framework. These activities will take place throughout the year, under nearly all conditions, and are more or less independent of the exterior environment. The participants have no choice.

optional activities
– only under favorable
exterior conditions

Optional activities – that is, those pursuits that are participated in if there is a wish to do so and if time and place make it possible – are quite another matter.

9

three types of outdoor activities

Necessary activities

Optional activities

Social activities

This category includes such activities as taking a walk to get a breath of fresh air, standing around enjoying life, or sitting and sunbathing.

These activities take place only when exterior conditions are favourable, when weather and place invite them. This relationship is particularly important in connection with physical planning because most of the recreational activities that are especially pleasant to pursue outdoors are found precisely in this category of activities. These activities are especially dependent on exterior physical conditions.

outdoor activities and quality of outdoor space

When outdoor areas are of poor quality, only strictly necessary activities occur.

When outdoor areas are of high quality, necessary activities take place with approximately the same frequency – though they clearly tend to take a longer time, because the physical conditions are better. In addition, however, a wide range of optional activities will also occur because place and situation now invite people to stop, sit, eat, play, and so on.

In streets and city spaces of poor quality, only the bare minimum of activity takes place. People hurry home.

In a good environment, a completely different, broad spectrum of human activities is possible.

| | Quality of the physical environment | |
	Poor	Good
Necessary activities	●	●
Optional activities	·	⬤
"Resultant" activities (Social activities)	●	●

Graphic representation of the relationship between the quality of outdoor spaces and the rate of occurrence of outdoor activities.

When the quality of outdoor areas is good, optional activities occur with increasing frequency. Furthermore, as levels of optional activity rise, the number of social activities usually increases substantially.

social activities

Social activities are all activities that depend on the presence of others in public spaces. Social activities include children at play, greetings and conversations, communal activities of various kinds, and finally – as the most widespread social activity – passive contacts, that is, simply seeing and hearing other people.

Different kinds of social activities occur in many places: in dwellings; in private outdoor spaces, gardens, and balconies; in public buildings; at places of work; and so on; but in this context only those activities that occur in publicly accessible spaces are examined.

These activities could also be termed "resultant" activities, because in nearly all instances they evolve from activities linked to the other two activity categories. They develop in connection with the other activities because people are in the same space, meet, pass by one another, or are merely within view.

Social activities occur spontaneously, as a direct consequence of people moving about and being in the same spaces. This implies that social activities are indirectly supported whenever necessary and optional activities are given better conditions in public spaces.

Greeting old friends, Bilbao

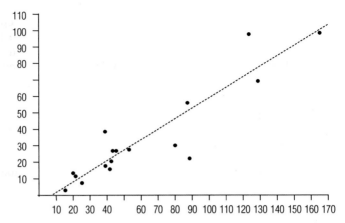

The more time people spend out-doors, the more frequently they meet and the more they talk. Chart plotting the relationship between the number of outdoor activities and frequency of interactions. (Street life sudies in Melbourne [20]. See also page 191.)

The character of social activities varies, depending on the context in which they occur. In the residential streets, near schools, near places of work, where there are a limited number of people with common interests or backgrounds, social activities in public spaces can be quite comprehensive: greetings, conversations, discussions, and play arising from common interests and because people "know" each other, if for no other reason than that they often see one another.

In city streets and city centers, social activities will generally be more superficial, with the majority being passive contacts – seeing and hearing a great number of unknown people. But even this modest type of activity can be very appealing.

Very freely interpreted, a social activity takes place every time two people are together in the same space. To see and hear each other, to meet, is in itself a form of contact, a social activity. The actual meeting, merely being present, is furthermore the seed for other, more comprehensive forms of social activity.

This connection is important in relation to physical planning. Although the physical framework does not have a direct influence on the quality, content, and intensity of social contacts, architects and planners can affect the possibilities for meeting, seeing, and hearing people – possibilities that both take on a quality of their own and become important as background and starting point for other forms of contact.

This is the background for the investigation in this book of meeting possibilities and opportunities to see and hear other people. Another reason for a comprehensive review of these activities is that precisely the presence of other people, activities, events, inspiration, and stimulation comprise one of the most important qualities of public spaces altogether.

13

life between buildings
– defined

If we look back at the street scene that was the starting point for defining the three categories of outdoor activities, we can see how necessary, optional, and social activities occur in a finely interwoven pattern. People walk, sit, and talk. Functional, recreational, and social activities intertwine in all conceivable combinations. Therefore, this examination of the subject of outdoor activities does not begin with a single, limited category of activities. Life between buildings is not merely pedestrian traffic or recreational or social activities. Life between buildings comprises the entire spectrum of activities, which combine to make communal spaces in cities and residential areas meaningful and attractive.

Both necessary, functional activities and optional, recreational activities have been examined quite thoroughly over the years in different contexts. Social activities and their interweaving to form a communal fabric have received considerably less attention.

This is the background for the following, more detailed examination of social activities in public spaces.

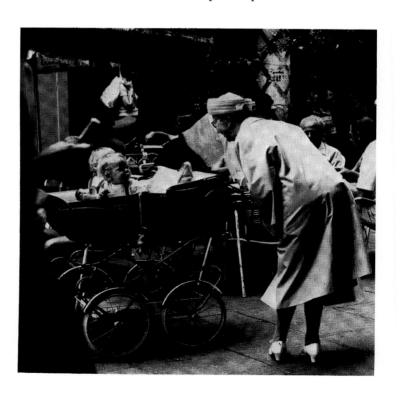

*Contact at a modest level
– but definitely contact.*

14

Life Between Buildings

life between buildings
– and the need for
contact

It is difficult to pinpoint precisely what life between buildings means in relation to the *need for contact* [14].

Opportunities for meetings and daily activities in the public spaces of a city or residential area enable one to be among, to see, and to hear others, to experience other people functioning in various situations.

These modest "see and hear contacts" must be considered in relation to other forms of contact and as part of the whole range of social activities, from very simple and noncommittal contacts to complex and emotionally involved connections.

The concept of varying degrees of contact intensity is the basis of the following simplified outline of various contact forms.

High intensity ↑   Close friendships
  Friends
  Acquaintances
  Chance contacts
  Passive contacts ("see and hear"
Low intensity   contacts)

In terms of this outline life between buildings represents primarily the low-intensity contacts located at the bottom of the scale. Compared with the other contact forms, these contacts appear insignificant, yet they are valuable both as independent contact forms and as prerequisites for other, more complex interactions.

Opportunities related to merely being able to meet, see, and hear others include:

  – contact at a modest level
  – a possible starting point for contact at other levels
  – a possibility for maintaining already established contacts
  – a source of information about the social world outside
  – a source of inspiration, an offer of stimulating experience

15

a possible beginning for contacts at other levels

Contact at a modest level.

– a form of contact

The possibilities related to the low-intensity contact forms offered in public spaces perhaps can best be described by the situation that exists if they are lacking.

If activity between buildings is missing, the lower end of the contact scale also disappears. The varied transitional forms between being alone and being together have disappeared. The boundaries between isolation and contact become sharper – people are either alone or else with others on a relatively demanding and exacting level.

Life between buildings offers an opportunity to be with others in a relaxed and undemanding way. One can take occasional walks, perhaps make a detour along a main street on the way home or pause at an inviting bench near a front door to be among people for a short while. Or one can do daily shopping, even though it would be more practical to do it once a week. Even looking out of the window now and then, if one is fortunate enough to have something to look at, can be rewarding. Being among others, seeing and hearing others, receiving impulses from others, imply positive experiences, alternatives to being alone. One is not necessarily with a specific person, but one is, nevertheless, with others.

As opposed to being a passive observer of other people's experiences on television or video or film, in public spaces the individual himself is present, participating in a modest way, but most definitely participating.

an opportunity for maintaining established contacts

– a possible access to contact at other levels	Low-intensity contact is also a situation from which other forms of contact can grow. It is a medium for the unpredictable, the spontaneous, the unplanned.

These opportunities can be illustrated by examining how play activities among children get started.

Such situations can be arranged. Formalized play occurs at birthday parties and arranged play groups in schools. Generally, however, play is not arranged. It evolves when children are together, when they see others at play, when they feel like playing and "go out to play" without actually being certain that play will get started. The first prerequisite is being in the same space. Meeting.

Contacts that develop spontaneously in connection with merely being where there are others are usually very fleeting – a short exchange of words, a brief discussion with the next man on the bench, chatting with a child in a bus, watching somebody working and asking a few questions, and so forth. From this simple level, contacts can grow to other levels, as the participants wish. Meeting, being present in the same space, is in each of these circumstances the prime prerequisite.

– an uncomplicated opportunity to maintain already established contacts	The possibility of meeting neighbors and co-workers often in connection with daily comings and goings implies a valuable opportunity to establish and later maintain acquaintances in a relaxed and undemanding way.

Social events can evolve spontaneously. Situations are allowed to develop. Visits and gatherings can be arranged on short notice, when the mood dictates. It is equally easy to "drop by" or "look in" or to agree on what is to take place tomorrow if the participants pass by one another's front doors often and, especially, meet often on the street or in connection with daily activities around the home, place of work, and so on.

Frequent meetings in connection with daily activities increase chances of developing contacts with neighbors, a fact noted in many surveys. With frequent meetings friendships and the contact network are maintained in a far simpler and less demanding way than if friendship must be kept up by telephone and invitation. If this is the case, it is often rather difficult to maintain contact, because more is always demanded of the participants when meetings must be arranged in advance.

This is the underlying reason why nearly all children and a considerable proportion of other age groups maintain closer and more frequent contact with friends and acquaintances who live or work near them – it is the simplest way to stay "in touch."

19

information about the social environment

— information about the social environment

The opportunity to see and hear other people in a city or residential area also implies an offer of valuable information, about the surrounding social environment in general and about the people one lives or works with in particular.

This is especially true in connection with the social development of children, which is largely based on observations of the surrounding social environment, but all of us need to be kept up to date about the surrounding world in order to function in a social context.

Through the mass media we are informed about the larger, more sensational world events, but by being with others we learn about the more common but equally important details. We discover how others work, behave, and dress, and we obtain knowledge about the people we work with, live with, and so forth. By means of all this information we establish a confident relationship with the world around us. A person we have often met on the street becomes a person we "know."

— a source of inspiration

In addition to imparting information about the social world outside, the opportunity to see and hear other people can also provide ideas and inspiration for action.

We are inspired by seeing others in action. Children, for example, see other children at play and get the urge to join in, or they get ideas for new games by watching other children or adults.

— a uniquely stimulating experience

The trend from living to lifeless cities and residential areas that has accompanied industrialization, segregation of various city functions, and reliance on the automobile also has caused cities to become duller and more monotonous. This points up another important need, namely *the need for stimulation* [14].

Experiencing other people represents a particularly colorful and attractive opportunity for stimulation. Compared with experiencing buildings and other inanimate objects, experiencing people, who speak and move about, offers a wealth of sensual variation. No moment is like the previous or the following when people circulate among people. The number of new situations and new stimuli is limitless. Furthermore, it concerns the most important subject in life: people.

Living cities, therefore, ones in which people can interact with one another, are always stimulating because they are rich in experiences, in contrast to lifeless cities, which can scarcely avoid being poor in experiences and thus dull, no matter how many colors and variations of shape in buildings are introduced.

21

If life between buildings is given favorable conditions through sensible planning of cities and housing areas alike, many costly and often stilted and strained attempts to make buildings "interesting" and rich by using dramatic architectural effects can be spared.

Life between buildings is both more relevant and more interesting to look at in the long run than are any combination of colored concrete and staggered building forms.

Inevitably, life between buildings is richer, more stimulating, and more rewarding than any combination of architectural ideas.

Above: New housing complex, Paris.

Below: Everyday scene.

Facing page: Children, workmen, and contemporary architecture (Les Arcades du Lac, Paris, 1981; architect, Ricardo Bofill).

activity as attraction
The value of the many large and small possibilities that are attached to the opportunity of being in the same space as and seeing and hearing other people is underlined by a series of observations investigating people's reaction to the presence of other people in public spaces [15, 18, 24, 51].

Wherever there are people — in buildings, in neighborhoods, in city centers, in recreational areas, and so on — it is generally true that people and human activities attract other people. People are attracted to other people. They gather with and move about with others and seek to place themselves near others. New activities begin in the vicinity of events that are already in progress.

In the home we can see that children prefer to be where there are adults or where there are other children, instead of, for example, where there are only toys. In residential areas and in city spaces, comparable behavior among adults can be observed.

activity as attraction

If given a choice between walking on a deserted or a lively street, most people in most situations will choose the lively street. If the choice is between sitting in a private backyard or in a semiprivate front yard with a view of the street, people will often choose the front of the house where there is more to see (see page 38).

In Scandinavia an old proverb tells it all' "people come where people are."

activities and play habits

A series of investigations illustrates in more detail the interest in being in contact with others. Investigations of children's play habits in residential areas [28, 39] show that children stay and play primarily where the most activity is occurring or in places where there is the greatest chance of something happening.

Both in areas with single-family houses and in apartment house surroundings, children tend to play more on the streets, in parking areas, and near the entrances of dwellings than in the play areas designed for that purpose but located in backyards of single-family houses or on the sunny side of multi-story buildings, where there are neither traffic nor people to look at.

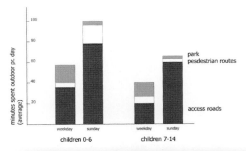

Even when well-developed systems of parks and pedestrian routes are available, children of all ages spend most of their time outdoors in or alongside the access roads. (Survey of children's play habits in single-family house areas in Denmark [29]).

activities and seating preferences

Below: All over the world sidewalk cafe chairs face the street life. (Photos from Karl Johan, main street, Oslo Norway)

Corresponding trends can be found regarding where people choose to sit in public spaces. Benches that provide a good view of surrounding activities are used more than benches with less or no view of others.

An investigation of Tivoli Garden in Copenhagen [36], carried out by the architect John Lyle, shows that the most used benches are along the garden's main path, where there is a good view of the particularly active areas, while the least used benches are found in the quiet areas of the park. In various places, benches are arranged back to back, so that one of the benches faces a path while the other "turns its back." In these instances it is always the benches facing the path that are used.

Comparable results have been found in investigations of seating in a number of squares in central Copenhagen. Benches with a view of the most trafficked pedestrian routes are used most, while benches oriented toward the planted areas of the squares are used less frequently [15, 18, 27].

At sidewalk cafes, as well, the life on the sidewalk in front of the cafe is the prime attraction. Almost without exception cafe chairs throughout the world are oriented toward the most active area nearby. Sidewalks are, not unexpectedly, the very reason for creating sidewalk cafes.

*When benches do not face
activities, either they will
not be used – or they will be
used in nontraditional ways*

REG: M 1.
DAG: M. 23.7.68,kl.12⁰⁰
VEJR: SMUKT, 20°C.
STÅENDE: 429   PERS.
SIDDENDE: 324   PERS.
IALT: 753   PERS.

attractions on a
pedestrian street

The opportunity to see, hear, and meet others can also be shown to be one of the most important attractions in city centers and on pedestrian streets. This is illustrated by an attraction analysis carried out on Strøget, the main pedestrian street in central Copenhagen, by a study group from the School of Architecture at the Royal Danish Academy of Fine Arts [15, 18]. The analysis was based on an investigation of where pedestrians stopped on the walking street and what they stopped to look at.

Fewest stops were noted in front of banks, offices, showrooms, and dull exhibits of, for example, cash registers, office furniture, porcelain, or hair curlers. Conversely, a great number of stops were noted in front of shops and exhibits that had a direct relationship to other people and to the surrounding social environment, such as newspaper kiosks, photography exhibits, film stills outside movie theaters, clothing stores, and toy stores.

Even greater interest was shown in the various human activities that went on in the street space itself. All forms of human activity appeared to be of major interest in this connection.

No one stops in front of banks and prestigious showrooms. Quite a few people stop to look at children's toys, photos, and other items related more directly to life and other people. By far the greatest number of people stop to watch other people and events.

28

Left: Registration of all people, standing and sitting, on the central part of the main pedestrian street in Copenhagen on a Tuesday in July at noon. Plan: 1:3000 [18].

Considerable interest was observed in both the ordinary, everyday events that take place on a street – children at play, newlyweds on their way from the photographers, or merely people walking by –and in the more unusual instance – the artist with his easel, the street musician with his guitar, street painters in action, and other large and small events.

It was obvious that human activities, being able to see other people in action, constituted the area's main attraction.

The street painters collected a large crowd as long as their work was in progress, but when they left the area, pedestrians walked over the paintings without hesitation. The same was true of music. Music blaring out on the street from loudspeakers in front of record shops elicited no reaction, but the moment live musicians began to play or sing, there was an instantaneous show of lively interest.

The attention paid to people and human activities was also illustrated by observations made in connection with the expansion of a department store in the area. While excavation and pouring of foundations were in progress, it was possible to see into the building site through two gates facing the pedestrian street. Throughout this period more people stopped to watch the work in progress on the building site than was the case for stops in front of all the department store's fifteen display windows together.

In this case, too, it was the workers and their work, not the building site itself, that was the object of interest. This was demonstrated further during lunch breaks and after quitting time – when no workers were on the site, practically nobody stopped to look.

life between buildings – one of the most important city attractions

A summary of observations and investigations shows that people and human activity are the greatest object of attention and interest. Even the modest form of contact of merely seeing and hearing or being near to others is apparently more rewarding and more in demand than the majority of other attractions offered in the public spaces of cities and residential areas.

Life in buildings and between buildings seems in nearly all situations to rank as more essential and more relevant than the spaces and buildings themselves.

Outdoor Activities
and Quality of Outdoor Space

life between buildings
– a planning
dimension

Life between buildings is discussed here because the extent and character of outdoor activities are greatly influenced by physical planning. Just as it is possible through choice of materials and colors to create a certain palette in a city, it is equally possible through planning decisions to influence patterns of activities, to create better or worse conditions for outdoor events, and to create lively or lifeless cities.

The spectrum of possibilities can be described by two extremes. One extreme is the city with multistory buildings, underground parking facilities, extensive automobile traffic, and long distances between buildings and functions. This type of city can be found in a number of North American and "modernized" European cities and in many suburban areas.

In such cities one sees buildings and cars, but few people, if any, because pedestrian traffic is more or less impossible, and because conditions for outdoor stays in the public areas near buildings are very poor. Outdoor spaces are large and impersonal. With great distances between buildings, there is nothing much to experience outdoors, and the few activities that do take place are spread out in time and space. Under these conditions most residents prefer to remain indoors in front of the television or on their balcony or in other comparably private outdoor spaces.

Another extreme is the city with reasonably low, closely spaced buildings, accommodation for foot traffic, and good areas for outdoor stays along the streets and in direct relation to residences, public buildings, places of work, and so forth. Here it is possible to see buildings, people coming and going, and people stopping in outdoor areas near the buildings because the outdoor spaces are easy and inviting to use. This city is a living city, one in which spaces inside buildings are supplemented with usable outdoor areas, and where public spaces have a much better chance of working well.

quality improvements – in city streets

Each quality improvement in the city of Copenhagen has been closely followed by an increase in the use of the public spaces. The improvements have – literally speaking – given room to a much wider range of human activities. While the city population has not increased the interest in using public spaces passively and actively definitely has.

1968
20,500 m² pedestrian area

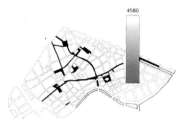

1986
55,000 m² pedestrian area

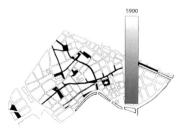

1995
71,000 m² pedestrian area

It has already been mentioned that the outdoor activities that are particularly dependent on the quality of the outdoor spaces are the optional, recreational activities, and by implication, a considerable part of the social activities. It is these specially attractive activities that disappear when conditions are poor and that thrive where conditions are favorable.

The significance of quality improvement to daily and social activities in cities can be observed where pedestrian streets or traffic-free zones have been established in existing urban areas. In a number of examples, improved physical conditions have resulted in impressive increases in the number of pedestrians, a lengthening of the average time spent outdoors, and a considerably broader spectrum of outdoor activities [17].

In a survey recording all activities occurring in the center of Copenhagen during the spring and summer of 1986, it was found that the number of pedestrian streets and squares in the city center had tripled between 1968 and 1986. Parallel to this improvement of the physical conditions, a tripling in the number of people standing and sitting was recorded.

A follow-up survey completed in 1995 recorded still more increases of activity in areas set aside for public life.

Facing page:
Average number of people engaged in stationary activities throughout the city centre at any time between noon and 4 pm on summer days in 1968, 1986 and 1995.

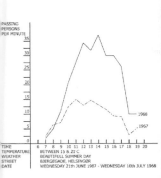

Pedestrian traffic before and after closing a street to vehicular traffic. (Bjerggade, Elsinore, Denmark [17].)

33

Entrance area to New York office building before and after quality improvement. (The Project for Public Spaces, New York, 1976 [42].)

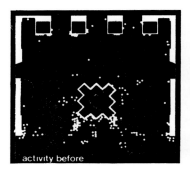

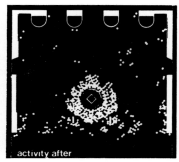

activity before

activity after

In cases where neighboring cities offer varying conditions for city activities, great differences can also be found.

In Italian cities with pedestrian streets and automobile-free squares, the outdoor city life is often much more pronounced than in the car-oriented neighboring cities, even though the climate is the same.

A 1978 survey of street activities in both trafficked and pedestrian streets in Sydney, Melbourne, and Adelaide, Australia, carried out by architectural students from the University of Melbourne and the Royal Melbourne Institute of Technology found a direct connection between street quality and street activity. In addition, an experimental improvement of increasing the number of seats by 100 percent in central Melbourne streets resulted in an 88 percent increase in seated activities.

William H. Whyte, in his book *The Social Life of Small Urban Spaces* [51], describes the close connection between qualities of city space and city activities and documents how often quite simple physical alterations can improve the use of the city space noticeably.

Comparable results have been achieved in a number of improvement projects executed in New York and other U.S. cities by the Project for Public Spaces [41].

In residential areas as well, both in Europe and the United States, traffic reduction schemes, courtyard clearing, laying out of parks, and comparable outdoor improvements have had a marked effect.

outdoor activities and quality deterioration

Conversely, the effect of the deterioration of quality on activities in ordinary residential streets is illustrated by the now very famous study of three neighboring streets in San Francisco, carried out in 1970–71 by Appleyard and Lintell [24],

The study shows the dramatic effect of increased traffic in two of the streets, all of which formerly had a modest rate of traffic.

In the street where there was only little traffic (2,000 vehicles per day), a great number of outdoor activities were registered. Children played on sidewalks and in the streets. Entranceways and steps were used widely for outdoor stays, and an extensive network of neighbor contacts was noted.

In one of the other streets, where the traffic volume was greatly increased (16,000 vehicles per day), outdoor activities became practically nonexistent. Comparably, neighbor contacts in this street were poorly developed.

In the third street, with middle to high traffic intensity (8,000 vehicles per day), a surprisingly great reduction in outdoor activities and neighbor contacts was noted, emphasizing that even a relatively limited deterioration of the quality of the outdoor environment can have a disproportionately severe negative effect on the extent of outdoor activities.

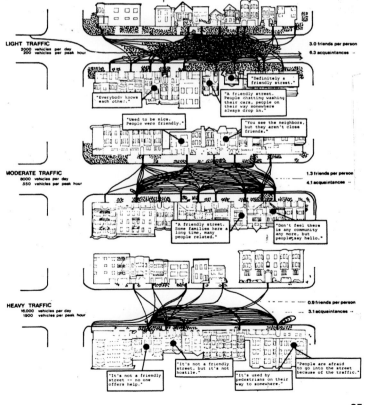

Registration of frequency of occurrence of outdoor activities (dots) and contacts between-friends and acquaintances (lines) in three parallel streets in San Francisco.
Above: Street with light traffic.
Center: Street with moderate traffic.
Below: Street with heavy traffic. Almost no outdoor activities and few friendships and acquaintances among the residents.
(From Appleyard and Lintell: "The Environmental Quality of City Streets" [4].)

freeing the restricted possibilities

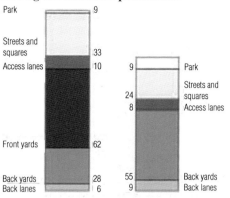

	GALGEBAKKEN		HYLDESPJÆLDET

Park — 9
Streets and squares — 33
Access lanes — 10
Front yards — 62
Back yards — 28
Back lanes — 6

Park — 9
Streets and squares — 24
Access lanes — 8
Back yards — 55
Back lanes — 9

G

H

Two housing areas located next to each other, just south of Copenhagen. Both areas were built 1973-75 and are inhabited by comparable groups. Galgebakken (area G), has a markedly better designed and detailed arrangement of outdoor spaces compared to the area below, Hyldespjældet (area H).
All dwellings in area G have a private backyard as well as a semiprivate front yard, whereas the dwellings in area H are provided with a backyard only.
A study of all outdoor activities in both areas taking place on Saturdays in the summer months of 1980 and 1981 showed that outdoor activities occurred at a 35 percent higher rate in area G. Front-yard activities in area G were found to be the determining factor for this substantial difference.
Above: Plan of the two areas 1:12,500.
Top: Access lane with front yards, area G.
Bottom: Access lane, area H.

how many, how long, and which activity

In summarizing the studies, a close relationship between outdoor quality and outdoor activities can be noted.

In at least three areas, it appears possible, in part through the design of the physical environment, to influence the activity patterns in public spaces in cities and residential areas. Within certain limits – regional, climatic, societal – it is possible to influence *how many* people and events use the public spaces, *how long* the individual activities last, and which activity types can develop.

freeing the restricted possibilities

The fact that a marked increase of outdoor activities is often seen in connection with quality improvements emphasizes that the situation found in a specific area at a certain time frequently gives an incomplete indication of the need for public spaces and outdoor activities, which can indeed exist in the area. The establishment of a suitable physical framework for social and recreational activities has time after time revealed a suppressed human need that was ignored at the outset.

When the main street in Copenhagen was converted to a pedestrian street in 1962 as the first such scheme in Scandinavia, many critics predicted that the street would be deserted because "city activity just doesn't belong to the northern European tradition." Today this major pedestrian street, plus a number of other pedestrian streets later added to the system, are filled to capacity with people walking, sitting, watching events, playing music, and talking together. It is evident that the initial fears were unfounded and that city life in Copenhagen had been so limited because there was previously no physical possibility for its existence.

In a number of new Danish residential areas as well, where physical possibilities for outdoor activity have been established in the form of high-quality public spaces, activity patterns that no one had believed possible in Danish residential areas have evolved.

Just as it has been noted that automobile traffic tends to develop concurrently with the building of new roads, all experience to date with regard to human activities in cities and in proximity to residences seems to indicate that where a better physical framework is created, outdoor activities tend to grow in number, duration, and scope.

The Middle Ages – physical and social aspects

In cities throughout Europe, medieval urban spaces are exceptionally well suited to urban outdoor activities by virtue of their spatial qualities and ample dimensioning. Urban spaces from later periods are much less successful in this respect, generally tending to be too large, too wide, and too straight.
Left: Rothenburg ob der Tauber, a well-preserved medieval city in southern Germany.

Martina Franca, Apulia, southern Italy. The differences between the spontaneously derived and the planned areas are evident. The intimate knowledge of human scale that characterizes medieval cities cannot be found in the newer, professionally planned urban areas.

Outdoor Activities and Architectural Trends

life between buildings
– and urban planning
ideology

Having noted in the preceding chapters a number of positive qualities related to life between buildings and having demonstrated that the scope and character of outdoor activities are greatly influenced by the physical environment, it is natural for us to examine the extent to which urban planning principles and architectural trends of different historical periods have influenced outdoor activities and thus the social outdoor activities as well.

In Europe, well-preserved cities from nearly all periods within the last thousand years still exist. Freely evolved as well as planned medieval cities abound. Renaissance and baroque cities, cities from the early phases of industrialization, garden cities inspired by romanticism, and, not least, functionalistic, automobile-dominated cities of the past fifty years are manifold. Today it is possible to compare and evaluate these city layouts on a relatively uniform basis, because they are still in use.

With regard to form, seemingly great variations exist between the different city models, especially from an art-historical point of view, yet in reality only two noteworthy radical developments in connection with the present discussion of urban planning ideologies and outdoor activities have occurred: one in relation to the Renaissance, and one in relation to the functionalism movement.

The Middle Ages
– physical and social
aspects

Professional planning as it is known today, in which experts design the city on paper and in models, to build and deliver it later complete to the clients, has its historical origins in the Renaissance. Planning and planners did exist in some earlier periods, as evidenced by a number of Greek and Roman cities, but with the exception of a small group of planned late-medieval colonial cities, the cities that grew up in the period from around AD 500 to AD 1500 were not planned in the true sense. They developed where there was a need for them, shaped by the residents of the city in a direct city-building process.

Piazza del Campo, Siena, Italy

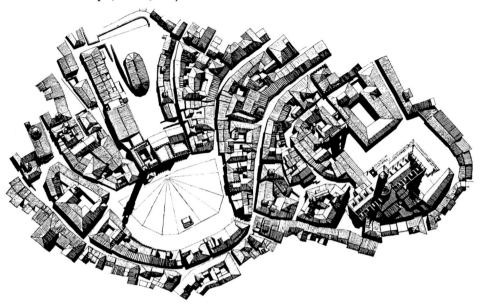

Above: City center, Siena, Italy.
Plan: 1:4000.

It is important to note that these cities did not develop based on plans but rather evolved through a process that often took many hundreds of years, because this slow process permitted continual adjustment and adaptation of the physical environment to the city functions. The city was not a goal in itself, but a tool formed by use.

The result of this process, which was based on a multitude of collected experiences, was urban spaces that even today offer extremely good conditions for life between buildings.

Many medieval cities and self-evolved small towns are increasingly popular as tourist attractions, objects of study, and desirable residential cities in contemporary times because they have precisely these qualities.

By virtue of their evolution, these cities and city spaces have built-in qualities that are found only in a few exceptional cases in cities from later periods. Nearly all medieval towns illustrate this. Not only are the streets and squares arranged with concern for people moving about and staying outdoors, but the city builders appear to have had remarkable insight concerning the fundamentals for this planning.

An unusually fine example is the Piazza del Campo in Siena. With its enclosed spatial design, its orientation with regard to sun and climate, its bowl-formed section, and its meticulously placed fountains and bollards, it is ideally arranged to function as a meeting place and public living room for its citizens, both then and now.

The Renaissance
– the visual aspects

Twice since the Middle Ages has the basis for city planning been radically changed.

The first radical change took place during the Renaissance and has direct relation to the transition from freely evolved to planned cities. A special group of professional planners assumed the work of building cities and developed theories and ideas about how cities ought to be.

The city was no longer merely a tool but became to a greater degree a work of art, conceived, perceived, and executed as a whole. No longer were the areas between buildings and the functions to be contained in them the major points of interest, but rather the spatial effects, the buildings, and the artists who had shaped them took precedence.

In this period it was primarily the appearance of the city and its buildings – the visual aspects – that were developed and transformed into criteria for good architecture and urban design. Concurrently, certain functional aspects were examined,

The Renaissance – the visual aspects

Left: Palmanova, Italy (1593). City plan in bird's-eye perspective.
Below: Eighteenth-century royal park in Drottningholm, Sweden, and central axis in a Danish public housing development (1965).

in particular the problems involved with defense, transportation, and formalized social functions such as parades and processions. The most important development in the basis for planning, however, concerned the visual expression of cities and buildings.

In Palmanova, the star-formed Renaissance city built by Scamozzi in 1593 north of Venice, all the streets have the same width – 14 meters (46 ft.) – regardless of purpose and placement in the city plan. In contrast with the medieval town, these dimensions are not determined primarily by use but by other, mostly formal considerations. This is also true of the city square, Piazza Grande, which, because of the geometry, is 30,000 square meters (325,000 sq.ft.) or more than twice as large as the Campo in Siena. For this reason it is quite unusable as a town square in this little town. On the other hand, the city plan is an interesting graphic work that, like so many other Renaissance-inspired plans, bears witness to being created on the drawing board.

The conscious awareness of the visual aspects of city planning during this period and the aesthetics formulated in this context decisively formed the basis for the architectural treatment of these problems in succeeding centuries.

functionalism
– the physiological,
functional aspect

The second important development of the basis for planning took place around 1930 under the name of functionalism. During this period the physical-functional aspects of cities and buildings were developed as a planning dimension independent from and supplementary to aesthetics.

The basis for functionalism was primarily the medical knowledge that had been developed during the 1800s and the first decades of the 1900s. This new and extensive medical knowledge was the background for a number of criteria for healthy and physiologically suitable architecture around 1930. Dwellings were to have light, air, sun, and ventilation, and the residents were to be assured access to open spaces. The requirements for detached buildings oriented toward the sun and not, as they had been previously, toward the street, and the requirement for separation of residential and work areas were formulated during this period in order to assure the individual healthy living conditions and to distribute the physical benefits more fairly.

"If we will demand residences of equally high hygienic standard for all, then the requirement of direct access to sunlight for all dwellings will come to give the new residential

functionalism – the physiological functional aspects

Top: Emphasis on sun, light, and open spaces and the elimination of public urban spaces are clearly expressed in the illustrations accompanying the functionalistic manifesto of Le Corbusier. ("Concerning Town Planning" [36]).
Center: Condominiums in Toronto, Canada.
Below: Public housing in Berlin.

areas a completely new character. It is, therefore, a necessity to have an open building principle with parallel buildings positioned according to the sun: east-west in the case of through-going apartments, otherwise north-south. The first-named type of building has, however, the advantage in that it permits cross ventilation and gives the residences a truly effective sunny side [2]." G. Asplund in *Acceptera*, 1930.

the streets that disappeared

The functionalists made no mention of the psychological and social aspects of the design of buildings or public spaces. This lack of interest is also evident regarding the public spaces. That building design could influence play activities, contact patterns, and meeting possibilities, to name a few examples, was not considered. Functionalism was a distinctly physically and materially oriented planning ideology. One of the most noticeable effects of this ideology was that streets and squares disappeared from the new building projects and the new cities.

Throughout the entire history of human habitation, streets and squares had formed focal points and gathering places, but with the advent of functionalism, streets and squares were literally declared unwanted. Instead, they were replaced by roads, paths, and endless grass lawns.

the "late modern" planning basis

In simplified form, the aesthetics formulated in the Renaissance and further developed in the following centuries, and the functionalist teachings regarding the physiological aspects of planning are the ideologies on which cities and housing have been built in the years from 1930 and right up to the last decades of the twentieth century. These concepts have been thoroughly examined in past years and made specific in regulations and building codes. And it is these concepts around which an important part of the work of architects and planners has been centered during these most important decades when the majority of all construction in the industrial countries has taken place.

social possibilities in physically oriented planning

In the 1930s no one could visualize how it would be to live in the new cities when the architects' aesthetics and the functionalistic ideas of healthy buildings became realities.

As an alternative to the existing dark, overpopulated, and unhealthy workers' housing, the new, light multistory blocks offered many obvious advantages, and it was easy to argue in their favor.

In the functionalistic manifestos the "romantic languishing" in the old cities was energetically addressed.

The consequences for the social environment were not discussed, because it was not recognized that buildings also had great influence on outdoor activities and consequently on a number of social possibilities. No one wished to reduce or exclude valuable social activities. On the contrary, it was thought that the extensive grass areas between the buildings would be the obvious location for many recreational activities and a rich social life. Perspective drawings teemed with life and activities. The extent to which these visions of the function of green spaces as the uniting element in building projects were correct was not challenged or investigated.

Not until twenty to thirty years later, in the 1960s and 1970s, when the big functionalistic multistory residential cities had been built, was it possible to evaluate the consequences of a one-sided physical-functional planning basis.

A review of just a small selection of the most common planning principles from functionalistic building projects illustrates the effects of this type of planning in relation to life between buildings.

functionalistic
planning versus life
between buildings

The spreading and thinning out of dwellings assured light and air but also caused an excessive thinning of people and events. Differentiation in function among dwellings, factories, public buildings, and so on may have reduced the physiological disadvantages, but it has also reduced the possible advantages of closer contact.

Great distances between people, events, and functions characterize the new city areas. Transportation systems, based on the automobile, further contributed to reducing outdoor activities. In addition, the mechanical and insensitive spatial design of individual building projects has had a dramatic effect on outdoor activities.

The term "desert planning" introduced by Gordon Cullen in his book *Townscape* [10] most accurately describes the consequences of functionalistic planning.

single-family housing
areas – life around
but not between
buildings

Parallel to the development of functionalistic multistory buildings, low, open, single-family housing areas, made possible by the increased use of automobiles, have been extensively developed in a number of countries, including Scandinavia, the United States, Canada, and Australia.

In these areas desirable conditions have been created in the form of gardens for private outdoor activities; at the same time communal outdoor activities have been reduced to a

bare minimum because of street design, automobile traffic, and especially the wide dispersal of people and events. In these areas the mass media and shopping centers have become virtually the only contact points with the outside world because life between buildings has been phased out.

life is built out of the new city areas

These examples illustrate how postwar planning has significantly influenced life between buildings. Life has literally been built out of these new areas, not as a part of a well-thought-out planning concept but as a by-product of a long series of other considerations.

While the medieval city with its design and dimensions collected people and events in streets and squares and encouraged pedestrian traffic and outdoor stays, the functionalistic suburban areas and building projects do precisely the opposite.

47

These new areas reinforce the reduction and spreading of outdoor activities that over the same span of years resulted from changes in industrial production and from a number of other social conditions.

If a team of planners at any time had been given the task of doing what they could to reduce life between buildings, they hardly could have achieved more thoroughly what has inadvertently been done in the sprawling suburban areas, as well as in numerous functionalist redevelopment schemes.

The post modern revolt against the rigidity of modernism has produced a great number of strained and stilted buildings designed with a greater emphasis on artistic statement than on the usefulness to the inhabitants.
On the other hand it has been demonstrated in a number of cases that contemporary architecture can cater to and enhance the daily life in and between buildings. Care and consideration in the design process make all the difference.

Above: New housing project. Rotterdam, Holland.
Below: Kresge College, Santa Cruz, California, built around a carefully laid out street. (Architects: Charles Moore and W. Turnbull.)

Life Between Buildings
– in Current Social Situations

active participation or passive consumption

It is hardly a coincidence that criticism of functionalism, of the new urban areas, and of the sprawling suburbs primarily has been directed specifically toward the neglected, the destroyed, and the missing public spaces.

The telephone, television, video, home computers, and so forth have introduced new ways of interacting. Direct meetings in public spaces can now be replaced by indirect electronic communication. Active presence, participation, and experience can now be substituted with passive picture watching, seeing what others have experienced elsewhere. The automobile has made it possible to replace active participation in spontaneous local social activities with a drive to see selected friends and attractions.

Abundant possibilities do exist for compensating for what has been lost. Precisely for this reason, the fact that there is still widespread critisism of the neglected public spaces is indeed thought provoking.

Something is missing.

protests

That something is missing is illustrated emphatically by widespread popular protests against physical planning as it is practiced, evidenced in debates on city and residential environments and the organization of residents around demands for improvement of the physical environment. Typical demands include better conditions for pedestrian and bicycle traffic, better conditions for children and the elderly and a better framework in general for recreational and social community functions.

projects

That something is missing has been expressed by a new generation of architects and planners in a strong clash with modernism and the sprawling suburbs [30, 34,]. The very revival of the city as a major architectural objective, including the careful planning of public spaces – streets, squares, parks – interprets and channels the wave of popular protest.

That something is missing has been further emphasized in recent years by a number of developmental trends in western industrial society [9].

Family patterns change. The average family size has decreased. In Scandinavia it is down to 2.2 people. The demand for easily accessible social opportunities outside the home is growing accordingly. The composition of the population is changing as well. In general there are fewer children and more adults. The situation in which 20 percent of the population is composed of old people, in good health, with ten, twenty, or even thirty years to enjoy after retirement, is becoming common in many industrial countries. In Scandinavia, this population group, which has a great deal of free time, is the most frequent user of city spaces. If the spaces are worth using, they are used.

Finally, the situation in the workplace also is changing rapidly. Many jobs have been emptied of social and creative contents by technology and efficiency measures. And technological development usually means a reduction of both the work load and the amount of time spent at work. More people have more time, and at the same time a number of social and creative needs must be satisfied through outlets other than the traditional workplace.

The residential area, the city, and the public spaces – from the community center to the main square – form a possible physical framework for satisfying a number of these new demands.

new street life patterns

The changed conditions in urban societies are expressed most clearly by recent changes in street life patterns.

Throughout the world automobile-dominated city centers have been transformed into pedestrian street systems. Life in the public spaces has increased markedly, well above and beyond the extended commercial activities. A comprehensive social and recreational city life has developed.

In Copenhagen, for example, the transformation began in 1962. Since then, more and more pedestrian streets have been created. City life has, year by year, grown in scope, in creativity, and in ingenuity [16]. Various folk festivals and a huge, very popular carnival have emerged. Nobody had believed such events were possible in Scandinavia. Now they exist because they are needed. Even more important, everyday activities have grown in scope and number. A 1995 survey of street life in downtown Copenhagen reveals a quadrupling of social and recreative activities over the past two decades. The city has not grown in this period, but definitely street life has.

Comparably, public spaces in new residential areas are used more when these spaces have the requisite quality. The public spaces are needed. The need for spaces of all types and sizes is obvious – from the little residential street to the city square.

life between buildings – an independent quality, and perhaps a beginning

Criticisms, reactions, and visions concerning the improvement of living conditions and cities form the basis for the following examination of the physical framework for life between buildings.

As a starting point, no comprehensive, ambitious program will be outlined. On the contrary, it is a prime concept that everyday life, ordinary situations, and spaces in which daily life is lived must form the center of attention and effort. This concept is expressed by three modest, yet fairly broad requirements of public spaces:

– desirable conditions for the necessary outdoor activities
– desirable conditions for the optional, recreational activities
– desirable conditions for the social activities

To be able to move about easily and confidently, to be able to linger in cities and residential areas, to be able to take pleasure in spaces, buildings, and city life, and to be able to meet and get together with other people – informally or in more organized fashion – these are fundamental to good cities and good building projects today, as in the past.

The importance of these requirements cannot be overestimated. They are modest demands that aim for a better and more useful framework for everyday activities. On the other hand, a good physical framework for life between buildings and for communal activities is, in all circumstances, a valuable, independent quality, and – perhaps – a beginning.

51

2. PREREQUISITES FOR PLANNING

Processes and Projects
Senses, Communication and Dimensions
Life Between Buildings – A Process

Processes and Projects

processes
– and projects

The interaction between the physical environment and activities in outdoor public spaces is the subject of this book. Social activities in outdoor spaces are, necessarily, an integral part of this interplay.

Discussed in previous sections are opportunities for meeting others, to establish and maintain contacts, to chat with neighbors over hedges. Examples have been given of the direct correlation between the scope of outdoor activities and frequency of interaction among neighbors. The more residents are outdoors, the more often they meet – and the more greetings are exchanged and conversations develop.

There is, however, no basis for concluding directly from such examples that contact and close ties between neighbors develop more or less automatically, solely on the basis of certain definite building forms. More than architecture is needed for these interactions to develop. Design that is conducive to such interaction will, however, encourage it.

prerequisites for
community activities

In order for neighbor contacts and various forms of communal activities to develop beyond a superficial level, a meaningful common denominator will generally be called for – common background, common interests, or common problems.

This especially relates to the conditions that are necessary for deeper, more meaningful contacts.

In terms of the other, more modest and often more functional contacts, the physical framework undoubtedly plays a more crucial and direct role.

interaction between
processes and projects

Interaction between social activities in the public spaces and the social processs must, therefore, in all circumstances be viewed on several levels - taking into account the prerequisites that exist in individual areas and the varied interests and needs of different kinds of residents or users within the areas.

In any case it can be noted that the physical framework to a greater or lesser extent can influence the inhabitants' social situation.

The physical framework itself can be designed so that the desired contact forms are impeded or even made impossible. Architecture literally can stand in the way of desired activity patterns.

Conversely, the physical framework can also be designed to give a broader spectrum of available possibilities, so that processes and building projects are permitted to support one another. It is

When entrances, balconies, verandas, front yards and gardens are facing the access street, people can follow the life in the public space and will meet frequently in the course of their daily activities. This can be an important factor for building social networks. (Sibelius-parken, Copenhagen, Denmark. Architects: Fællestegnestuen)

The subdivision of housing schemes has become quite wide-spread in new Scandinavian residential areas.
The small housing group of 15-30 households has, in particular, been found to work quite well, encouraging social networking.
Right: Skaade, Denmark. 1985. (arch.: C.F. Møllers Tegnestue.)
Below: The neighborhood block as an organizing unit.

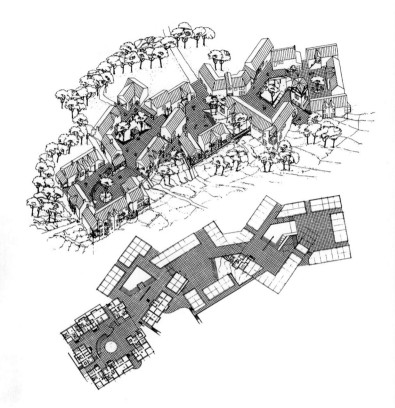

in this context that work with public spaces and life between buildings must be seen. Possibilities can be impeded – or they can be facilitated.

The following examples illustrate in greater detail practical attempts made to establish interaction between processes and building projects. A number of principles and definitions are also introduced.

social structure

The need to create subdivisions and groups in order to make democratic processes function is evident in places of work, associations, schools, and universities.

At universities, for example, a hierarchy exists consisting of faculties, institutes, departments, and finally, study groups, the smallest unit. The structure confers a decision-making rank and provides the individual with a series of social and professional points of reference.

interaction between process and project: Tinggården, Copenhagen

The cooperative housing project Tinggården, south of Copenhagen (built 1977-79), is subdivided into 6 housing groups (A through F), each with an average of 15 households. Each housing group is centered around a communal square and community house (2). The community center (1), shared by all the groups, is located on the main street.
(Architects Tegnestuen Vandkunsten)

Right: Housing group (A) organized around the two communal spaces: the outdoor square and the indoor community house.
Below: Plan 1:1750.

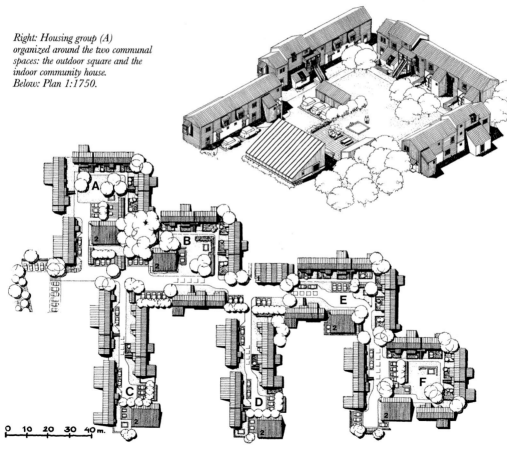

0 10 20 30 40 m.

social structure	The Danish cooperative housing project Tinggården [49], con-
– in the residential	sisting of eighty rental housing units built in 1978, is an example
context	of a building complex in which planners carefully considered

social structure
– in the residential
context

The Danish cooperative housing project Tinggården [49], consisting of eighty rental housing units built in 1978, is an example of a building complex in which planners carefully considered both social and physical structure. The goal was to get processes and project to work together.

Planning was a joint venture of the future residents and the architects and illustrates a clear attitude toward a desired social structure.

The building complex is divided into six groups of approximately fifteen individual housing units, each with a communal building.

In addition, there is a large community center for the entire complex. This hierarchical division – dwelling, dwelling group, housing complex, city – is motivated by the wish to strengthen the community and the democratic processes in the individual housing groups as well as in the housing development as a whole.

physical structure
– in the residential
context

The physical structure of the building complex reflects and supports the desired social structure.

The hierarchy of social groupings is reflected by a hierarchy of communal spaces: the family has a living room; residences are organized around two communal spaces, the outdoor square and the indoor communal house; and finally, the entire residential complex is built up around a public main street in which the large community center also is located. Family members meet in the living room, the inhabitants of the residential group meet in the group square, and residents from the entire neighborhood meet on the main street.

interaction between
process and project

The idea underlying this and comparable building projects is that the physical structure – the project – both visually and functionally supports the desired social structure of the residential area.

Visually, the social structure is expressed physically by placing the residences around group squares or group streets.

Functionally, the social structure is supported by establishing communal spaces, indoors and outdoors, at the various levels in the hierarchical structure.

The major function of the communal spaces is to provide the arena for life between buildings, the daily unplanned activities – pedestrian traffic, short stays, play, and simple social activities from which additional communal life can develop, as desired by the residents.

Diffuse structure. Suburban area, Melbourne, Australia.

diffuse structures

A counterpart to Tinggården, with its clear social and corresponding physical divisions, is the ordinary suburban single-family housing area or a multistory housing area.

The social structure here often consists of the family/household as the smallest unit. Between this unit and the very large unit – the city center or shopping center – only diffuse subdivision exists. Physically the structure performs in the same manner, without clear divisions. Residential areas have a diffuse interior structure and imprecise boundaries. It is not clear where the individual dwelling "belongs" or where the residential area "ends." The design of residential streets rarely takes into account where and how communal activities can take place at all. Under these conditions the undefined physical structure itself is a tangible obstacle to life between buildings.

The two housing examples illustrate the possibility of working with the concepts of social and physical structure in the housing context and emphasize how public spaces and life between buildings naturally must be seen in connection with social processes and group sizes. The examples also emphasize how life between buildings, meeting opportunities at the various levels, can enter into the efforts to develop and maintain the social processes.

degrees of privacy

In connection with the introduction of the hierarchical systems of communal spaces – from the living room to the city's town hall square – and the relationship of these spaces to various social groups, it is possible to define varying degrees to which different spaces are public and private.

At one end of the scale is the private residence with private outdoor space such as a garden or a balcony. The public spaces

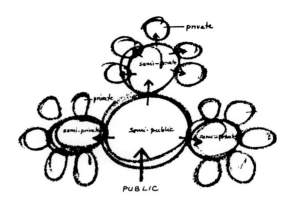

in the residential group are, it is true, publicly accessible, but have – because of close connection to a limited number of residences – a semipublic character. The communal spaces in the neighborhood are somewhat more public, while the city's town hall square is a totally public space.

The scale between public and private also can be considerably more differentiated than mentioned here. Or it can be considerably less defined, as in the case with the multistory residence or the single-family house in the undefined city structure. In many such cases, almost no middle ground or transition between private and very public territory exists.

territories, security, and sense of belonging

The establishment of a social structure and corresponding physical structure with communal spaces at various levels permits movement from small groups and spaces toward larger ones and from the more private to the gradually more public spaces, giving a greater feeling of security and a stronger sense of belonging to the areas outside the private residence. The area that the individual perceives as belonging to the dwelling, the residential environment, can extend well beyond the actual dwelling. This in itself may result in greater use of public spaces – such as parents permitting young children to play outdoors at an earlier age than they otherwise might.

Establishing residential areas so that there is a graduation of outdoor spaces with semipublic, intimate, and familiar spaces nearest the residence also makes it possible to know the people in the area better, and the experience of outdoor spaces as belonging to the residential area results in a greater degree of surveillance and collective responsibility for this public space and its residences. The public spaces become part of the residential

territories and sense of belonging

Hierarchical organization of residential area with clearly marked transitions between private and shared spaces. (From Oscar Newman, Defensible Space *[41].)*
A clear definition of borders is an important step in clarifying internal organization and solving local problems.
Below left: Clearly delineated entrances to housing groups (Byker, Newcastle upon Tyne.
Below right: Unofficial welcome sign by community group that advocates a subdivision of the city of Copenhagen: "24,000 inhabitants – ruled by Copenhagen."

habitat and are protected against vandalism and crime in the same way that the residences themselves are safeguarded [9, 40].

The importance of subdividing residential areas into smaller, better defined units as a link in more comprehensive hierarchical systems is increasingly recognized and is often used in new building projects. Several examples demonstrate that the residents in these small units are more quickly and more effectively able to organize themselves for group activities and to solve mutual problems.

Another area in which division of building projects into smaller, more clearly defined units is used to an increasing extent is in connection with renovation and improvement of existing areas. One of the most urgent problems in these older public housing areas relates to their size and the imprecisely defined public spaces, which, because they are too big and lack clarity, have the character of a no-man's-land.

transition zones
– gentle transitions

In conclusion mention should be made of flowing, gentle transitions between the various categories of public spaces. It is expedient and often important that transitions, for example, between city street and residential group, are indicated physically, but at the same time it is important that the indication is not so firm a demarcation that it prevents contacts with the outside world. For example, good visual connection is important so that a child can see whether playmates are out in the neighboring play area.

Good examples of well-thought-out social and physical structures and transitional zones that are clearly defined yet accessible and easy to traverse are found in Ralph Erskine's housing projects at Landskrona and Sandvika in Sweden and at Byker in Newcastle in Great Britain. [7]

The Byker complex is an urban renewal project in which 12,000 residents from an old, worn-out rowhouse area were relocated in new residences, built on the same site as the old structures were demolished. To ease the transfer and continuity from the old to the new buildings, great care was taken to divide the new project into clearly defined units – residential groups and city districts corresponding to the old streets and districts. Further, a precise physical demarcation of transitional zones was accomplished with portals and gates, so that individual residential groups are clearly defined; they do not, however, present such a solid boundary that it becomes unduly difficult to visit with others.

the senses and communication

Physical arrangement can promote or prevent visual and auditory contact in at least five different ways.

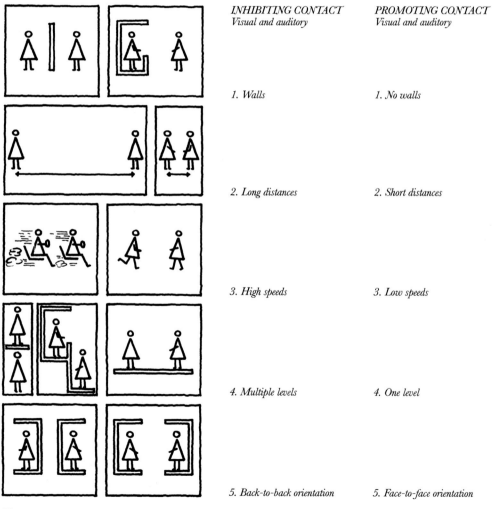

INHIBITING CONTACT *Visual and auditory*	PROMOTING CONTACT *Visual and auditory*
1. Walls	*1. No walls*
2. Long distances	*2. Short distances*
3. High speeds	*3. Low speeds*
4. Multiple levels	*4. One level*
5. Back-to-back orientation	*5. Face-to-face orientation*

Senses, Communication, and Dimensions

the senses
– a necessary
planning
consideration

Familiarity with human senses – the way they function and the areas in which they function – is an important prerequisite for designing and dimensioning all forms of outdoor spaces and building layouts.

Because sight and hearing are related to the most comprehensive of the outdoor social activities – seeing and hearing contacts – how they function is, naturally, a fundamental planning factor. A knowledge of the senses is a necessary prerequisite also in relation to understanding all other forms of direct communication and the human perception of spatial conditions and dimensions.

a frontal and
horizontal sensory
apparatus

Human movement is by nature limited to predominantly horizontal motion at a speed of approximately 5 kilometers per hour (3 mph), and the sensory apparatus is finely adapted to this condition. The senses are essentially frontally oriented, and one of the best developed and most useful senses, the sense of sight, is distinctly horizontal. The horizontal visual field is considerably wider than the vertical. If one looks straight ahead, it is possible to glimpse what is going on to both sides within a horizontal circle of almost ninety degrees to each side.

The downward field of vision is much narrower than the horizontal, and the upward field of vision is narrower still. The field of upward vision is reduced further because the axis of vision when walking is directed approximately ten degrees downward, in order to see where one is walking. A person walking down a street sees practically nothing but the ground floor of buildings, the pavement, and what is going on in the street space itself.

Events to be perceived must therefore take place in front of the viewer and on approximately the same level, a fact that is reflected in the design of all types of spectator spaces – theaters, movie houses, auditoriums. In theaters balcony tickets cost less because events cannot be seen in the "correct" way; and no one will accept sitting at a level lower than the stage floor. Another example that illustrates the vertical limitations of the field of vision is the merchandise display in supermarkets. Ordinary household products are placed below eye level, on the shelves nearest the floor, while the shelves in a narrow band just at eye level are filled with the unimportant, unnecessary goods that stores want customers to buy impulsively.

Everywhere that people move about and are engaged in activities, they do so on horizontal planes. It is difficult to move upward or downward, difficult to converse upward or downward, and difficult to look up or down.

distance receptors and immediate receptors

The anthropologist Edward T. Hall in his book *The Hidden Dimension* [23] gives a description of the most important senses and their functions in connection with human contacts and with experiencing the outside world. According to Hall, two categories of the sensory apparatus can be defined: the distance receptors — eyes, ears, nose — and the immediate receptors — skin, membranes, muscles. These receptors have different degrees of specialization and different functional spheres.

In the present context the distance receptors are of particular importance.

smell

The sense of smell registers variations in odors within a very limited range. Only at distances of less than 1 meter (39 in.) is it generally possible to catch the relatively weak odors emanating from the hair, skin, and clothing of other people. Perfume and other slightly stronger odors can be perceived at 2 to 3 meters (7 to 10 ft.). Beyond this distance human beings can perceive only much stronger smells.

hearing

The sense of hearing has a greater functional range. Within distances of up to 7 meters (23 ft.), the ear is quite effective. It is possible to hold conversations with relatively little difficulty up to this distance. At distances up to approximately 35 meters (100 ft.), it is still possible to hear a lecturer, for example, and establish a question-and-answer situation, but it is not possible to engage in actual conversations.

Beyond 35 meters (100 ft.), the ability to hear others is greatly reduced. It is possible to hear people who shout loudly but difficult to understand what is being shouted. If the distance is one kilometer (5/8 mi.) or more, it is only possible to hear very loud noises such as a cannon roar or a high-flying jet.

seeing	The sense of sight has an even wider functional area. It is possible to see the stars and often possible to see clearly airplanes that cannot be heard. In connection with experiencing other people, however, the sense of sight has, like the other senses, well-defined limitations.
the social field of vision – 0 to 100 meters (0 to 325 ft.)	One can see others and perceive that they are people at distance from ½ to 1 kilometer (1,600 to 3,200 ft.), depending on factors such as background, lighting, and particularly, whether or not the people in question are moving. At approximately 100 meters (325 ft.), figures that can be seen at greater distances become human individuals. This range can be called *the social field of vision*. An example of how behavior is affected by this range is the sparsely populated beach where individual groups of bathers distribute themselves at about 100-meter (325-ft.) intervals, as long as there is available space. At this distance the groups can perceive that there are others farther along the beach, but it is not possible to see who they are or what they are doing. At a distance of between 70 and 100 meters (250 and 325 ft.), it begins to be possible to determine with reasonable certainty a person's sex, approximate age, and what that person is doing.

At this distance it is often possible to recognize people one knows well on the basis of their clothing and the way they walk.

The 70- to 100-meter (250- to 325-ft.) limit also affects spectator situations in various sport arenas, such as football fields. The distance from the farthest seat to the middle of the field, for example, is usually 70 meters (250 ft.). Otherwise spectators cannot see what is going on.

Not until the distance is considerably shorter does it become possible to discern the details that permit one to perceive other people as individuals. At a distance of approximately 30 meters (100 ft.), facial features, hairstyle, and age can be seen and people met only infrequently can be recognized. When the distance is reduced to 20 to 25 meters (60 to 80 ft.), most people can perceive relatively clearly the feelings and moods of others. At this point the meeting begins to become truly interesting and relevant in a social context.

A related example is the theater. The distance between the stage and the farthest audience seats in a theater is usually a maximum of 30 to 35 meters (100 to 115 ft.). In theaters primarily feelings are communicated, and even though the actors are able to "enlarge" visual impressions by means of makeup and exaggerated movements, there are strict limits as to

seeing – a matter of distance

80 m (240 ft.)

7.5 m (25 ft.)

50 m (150 ft.)

2 m (6 ft.)

20 m (60 ft.)

40 cm (14 in.)

how far away the audience can sit if it is to get anything out of the performance.

At even shorter distances the amount and intensity of information is increased greatly because the other senses can now begin to supplement the sense of sight. At distances of 1 to 3 meters (3 to 10 ft.), at which normal conversations usually take place, the experience involves the degree of detail generally necessary for meaningful human contact. At still shorter distances, impressions and feelings are further intensified.

distances and
communication

The interplay between the intensity and distance of sensual impressions is widely used in human communication. The intense emotional contacts take place at quite close range, 0 to $\frac{1}{2}$ meters (0 to 2 ft.), where all the senses can work together and where all nuances and details can be perceived clearly, while the less intense contacts take place at greater distances, $\frac{1}{2}$ to 7 meters (2 to 20 ft.).

A very conscious use of distances is involved in nearly all contacts. The distance between participants is reduced if mutual interest and intensity are increased. People move closer together or lean forward in their chairs. The situation becomes "closer," more intense. Conversely, the distance is increased if interest and intensity wane. For example, the distance is increased when a discussion nears its end. If one of the participants wishes to end a conversation, he will step back a few steps – he "backs out of the situation."

In addition, language has numerous references to this connection between distance and intensity of contact. One speaks of "a close friendship," "a near relative," of "distant relations," "keeping somebody at arm's length," or "keeping one's distance from somebody."

This fact, that distance is used both to regulate intimacy and intensity in various social situations and to control the beginning and end of individual conversations, implies that a certain space is needed for conversations. Elevators, for example, are practically impossible spaces for ordinary conversations. The same is true of a front yard with a depth of 1 meter (3 ft.). In both these cases there is no way to avoid undesired contacts or to back out of undesired situations. On the other hand, where front yards are too deep, conversations cannot get started. Surveys in Australia, Canada, and Denmark (see pages 38 and 191) have demonstrated that a distance of $3\frac{1}{4}$ meters (10 ft.) appears to be very useful in this particular context.

small dimensions equal warm, intimate spaces

Distances are used to connote different relationships among people. Such phrases as "close friends" and "keeping an arm's distance from someone" indicate the degree of intimacy achieved. Correspondingly, small spaces tend to be perceived as warm and personal. The small dimensions make it possible to see and hear other people, and in small spaces, the details as well as the whole can be enjoyed. Conversely, large spaces are perceived as cold and impersonal. Buildings as well as people are "kept at a distance."

Left: London Court, Perth, Westaustralia.
Below: La Défense, Paris.

| social distances | In *The Hidden Dimension* [23] Edward T. Hall defines a number of *social distances*, that is to say, customary distances for different forms of communication in the Western European and American cultural sphere. |

Intimate distance (0 to 45 centimeters – 0 to 1½ ft.) is the distance at which intense feelings are expressed: tenderness, comfort, love, and also strong anger.

Personal distance (0.45 to 1.30 meters – 1½ to 4½ ft.) is the conversation distance between close friends and family. An example is the distance between people at the family dinner table.

Social distance (1.30 to 3.75 meters – 4½ to 12 ft.) is the distance for ordinary conversation among friends, acquaintances, neighbors, co-workers, and so on. The sofa group with armchairs and a coffee table is a physical expression of this social distance.

Finally, *public distance* (greater than 3.75 meters – 12 ft.) is defined as the distance used in more formal situations – around public figures or in teaching situations with one-way communication or when someone wants to hear or see an event but does not wish to become involved.

small and large dimensions

The relationship between distance and intensity, closeness and warmth, in various contact situations has an important parallel in the prevalent perception of architectural dimensions. In cities and building projects of modest dimensions, narrow streets, and small spaces, the buildings, building details, and the people who move about in the spaces are experienced at close range and with considerable intensity. These cities and spaces are comparably perceived as intimate, warm, and personal. Conversely, building projects with large spaces, wide streets, and tall buildings often are felt to be cold and impersonal.

time to experience

In addition to the requirement that objects and events be near eye level in order to be perceived, and to the requirements imposed by the limited range of human vision, another important factor in experiencing others is that there must be a reasonable amount of time in which to see and process visual impressions.

The organs of sense are for the most part designed to perceive and process the details and impressions that are received at walking and running speed, that is, 5 to 15 kilometers per hour (3 to 9 mph). If the speed of movement is increased, the possibility of discerning details and processing meaningful social information drops sharply. A somber illustration of this

69

car city scale/pedestrian city scale

The size of the cars and, especially, the speed of movement create substantial differences between automobile cities and pedestrian cities. In order to make buildings and signs visible to vehicular traffic, coarse design and huge symbols, are required.

Loud, coarse 50-mile-per-hour architecture is evident in American "burger strips," with their strained pizza palaces, gas stations, and oversized signals. However, the conflict between the two scales is present whenever fast and slow modes of traffic share the same spaces.

*Slow speeds, small dimensions,
and careful detailing are closely
interrelated.*
Above: Marken, Holland.
Right: Copenhagen, Denmark.

phenomenon can be observed on highways, where traffic often comes to a standstill in both lanes when there is an accident in one, because drivers in the other lane reduce their speed to 5 miles per hour to see what has happened. Another example is the slide presentation in which slides are changed too quickly, until the audience demands a slower tempo in order to "see what's going on."

When two people walk toward each other, approximately thirty seconds pass from the time they see or recognize each other until they meet. During this entire period, the mass of information and degree of detail perceived increase gradually, giving each person time to react to the situation. If this reaction time is critically reduced, the ability to perceive and respond to the situation disappears, as is the case when a car quickly passes a hitchhiker on the road.

**automobile city scale
– pedestrian city scale**

If people who move quickly are to be able to perceive objects and people, representations must be enlarged greatly.

Therefore the automobile city and the pedestrian city have quite different sizes and dimensions. In the automobile city, signs and billboards must be very big and bold to be seen. Buildings are comparably large and poor in detail, since these cannot be seen in any case. And the faces and facial expressions of human beings are too small in scale to be perceived at all.

71

life takes place on foot

It is important that all meaningful social activities, intense experiences, conversations, and caresses take place when people are standing, sitting, lying down, or walking. One can catch a brief glimpse of others from a car or from a train window, but life takes place on foot. Only "on foot" does a situation function as a meaningful opportunity for contact and information in which the individual is at ease and able to take time to experience, pause, or become involved.

physical planning for isolation and contact

If the possibilities and limitations related to the senses are summarized, it appears that there are five different means with which architects and planners either can promote or prevent isolation and contact.

isolation	contact
walls	no walls
long distances	short distances
high speeds	low speeds
multiple levels	one level
orientation away from others	orientation toward others

By working with these five principles individually or in combinations, it is possible to establish the physical prerequisites for isolation and contact, respectively.

Life takes place on foot.
(Pedestrian priority street,
Copenhagen, Denmark.)

Life Between Buildings – A Process

life between buildings
– a self-reinforcing
process

Life between buildings is potentially a self-reinforcing process. When someone begins to do something, there is a clear tendency for others to join in, either to participate themselves or just to experience what the others are doing. In this manner individuals and events can influence and stimulate one another. Once this process has begun, the total activity is nearly always greater and more complex than the sum of the originally involved component activities.

In the home, events and members of the family move gradually from room to room as the center of activity is changed. When work is going on in the kitchen, children play on the kitchen floor, and so forth.

On the playgrounds it can be noted how play activities are comparably self-reinforcing. If some children begin to play, others are inspired to come out and join in the games, and the little group can quickly grow. A process has begun.

In the public domain similar patterns can be seen. If there are many people, or if something is going on, more people and more events tend to join in, and the activities grow both in scope and duration.

one plus one is three
– at least

The Dutch architect F. van Klingeren, who has worked consciously with assembling and mixing various city activities in city centers in Dronten and Eindhoven in Holland [11], has observed how the entire activity level in these cities has increased as a consequence of such a self-reinforcing process.

Van Klingeren has summarized his experience of city activities in the formula "one plus one is three – at least."

the positive process:
something happens
because something
happens

A striking illustration of this principle has been found by studying patterns of children's play in areas consisting of single-family houses and rowhouses in Denmark [28]. In the rowhouse areas, the "density" of children per acre was found to be twice as

73

something happens because something happens

high as in the more spread-out areas of detached houses. In areas with twice the number of children, a four times higher level of play activity was found.

Something happens because something happens because something happens.

That life between buildings is a self-reinforcing process also helps to explain why many new housing developments seem so lifeless and empty. Many things go on, to be sure, but both people and events are so spread out in time and space that the individual activities almost never get a chance to grow together to larger, more meaningful and inspiring sequences of events. The process becomes negative: *nothing happens because nothing happens.*

Children would rather stay in and watch television because it is so dull outside. Old people do not find it particularly entertaining to sit on the benches, because there is almost nothing to see. And when there are few children playing, few people sitting on benches, and few walking by, it is not very interesting to look out of the windows. There is not much to see.

This negative process, in which life between buildings is drastically reduced because activities cannot stimulate and support one another, can, as mentioned, be found in the many suburban areas where there is an extreme dispersal of the events that actually do take place.

Comparable negative processes begin in connection with renovation of old city districts in which parking garages, gas stations, large financial institutions, and so on contribute to decreasing the number of people and events. The natural activity level in the streets, that is, the activities related to the daily life

Facing page: People tend to congregate where other people are assembled. Residential areas in western Copenhagen and southern Melbourne.

75

slow traffic means lively cities

The freeway and the pedestrian mall each have a traffic rate of 85 persons per minute. In the mall, however, more than twenty times as many people are in view at any specific time, because many people are sitting and standing, and because the speed of movement is 3 miles per hour rather than 60 miles per hour.

of the inhabitants, falls because the number of inhabitants is decreased, and the street environment deteriorates. The street assumes the character of a deserted no-man's-land, where nobody wants to be.

The disintegration of living public spaces and the gradual transformation of the street areas into an area that is of no real interest to anyone is an important factor contributing to vandalism and crime in the streets.

This development is found to a frightening extent in a number of large U.S. cities and is described by Jane Jacobs in her book *The Death and Life of Great American Cities* [24] and later further elaborated on by Oscar Newman in his book Defensible Space [40]. Nearly all large European cities are undergoing comparable developments.

Once crime or fear becomes a problem, everyone stays away from the streets - with good reason. The vicious circle is complete.

life between buildings
– a question of both
number and duration
of events

In connection with the effort to give the positive processes a chance, it is important to note that life between buildings, the people and events that can be observed in a given space, is a *product of number and duration of the individual events*. It is not the number of people or events, but rather the number of minutes spent outdoors that is important.

The following example illustrates this relationship.

If three people remain in front of their houses for sixty minutes each, throughout the period three people are present in the space. If thirty people each stay in front of their houses for six minutes, the activity level – the entire time spent outdoors – is the same (30 X 6 = 180 minutes). Within the period in question there will still be an average of three people present in the space.

The number of people or events does not, then, in itself give a real indication of the activity level in an area, because actual activity, life between buildings as it is experienced, is equally a question of duration of stays outdoors. This implies that a high level of activity in a certain area can be stimulated *both by ensuring that more people use the public spaces and by encouraging longer individual stays*.

slow traffic means
lively cities

If the speed of movement is reduced from 60 to 6 kilometers per hour (35 to 3.5 mph), the number of people on the streets will appear to be ten times greater, because each person will be within visual range ten times longer.

This is the prime reason for the noteworthy activity level in pedestrian cities like Dubrovnik and Venice. When all traffic is slow, there is life in the streets for this reason alone, in contrast to what is found in automobile cities, where the speed of movement automatically reduces the activity level.

Whether people move about on foot or in cars and whether cars, when used, are parked 5, 100, or 200 meters (15, 330, or 660 ft.) from the front door are determining factors regarding activities and opportunities for neighbors to meet one another.

The farther away from the doors the cars are parked, the more will happen in the area in question, because *slow traffic means lively cities*.

lengthy stays outdoors mean lively cities

Winter and summer scene from a street in Copenhagen. In the summer situation the street is much more lively, because nearly everyone is spending more time in the street. People are standing and sitting and the pace of walking is 20% slower than in the winter situation. Even with the same number of pedestrians per day the summer situation could easily result in 5 or 10 times more people present in the street because lengthy stays make lively cities.

lengthy stays
outdoors mean lively
residential areas and
city spaces

The duration of all functions in the public domain influences the activity level comparably.

If people are tempted to remain in the public spaces for a long time, a few people and a few events can grow to a considerable activity level.

If opportunities for outdoor activities in a residential area are improved so much that the average daily time spent outdoors is increased from ten to twenty minutes, the activity level in the area will be doubled.

When compared with the time used for transportation, the duration of the stay is by far the more important factor in this context.

While a change from car to foot traffic increases the average duration of each "trip" in the area by, perhaps, two minutes, an increase of the duration of stays outdoors from ten to twenty minutes will have a five times greater effect.

It is even more true than is the case for slow traffic that *lengthy stays outdoors mean lively residential areas and city spaces.*

This connection, that duration is as important as the number of events, explains in great part why there is so little activity in many new housing projects, such as multistory apartment areas, where great numbers of people in fact live. Residents come and go in great numbers, but there are often only meager opportunities to spend extended periods outdoors. There are not really any places to be, nothing to do. Thus outdoor stays become short, and the activity level is comparably low.

Rowhouses with small front yards may have considerably fewer inhabitants but much more activity around the houses because the period of time spent outdoors per inhabitant is generally much longer.

The connection demonstrated between street life, the number of people and events, and the time spent outdoors provides one of the most crucial keys to the way in which conditions for life between buildings can be improved in existing and new residential areas – namely by improving conditions for outdoor stays.

79

3. TO ASSEMBLE OR DISPERSE:
City and Site Planning

To Assemble or Disperse
To Integrate or Segregate
To Invite or Repel
To Open Up or Close In

 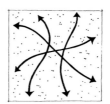

to assemble or
disperse

If activities and people are assembled, it is possible for individual events, as mentioned, to stimulate one another. Participants in a situation have the opportunity to experience and participate in other events. A self-reinforcing process can begin.

In this and the three following sections attention is drawn to a number of the planning decisions that influence the assembly or dispersal of people and events. This is a general examination of issues that must be considered in order to provide a basis for conscious planning in individual situations, whether the goal is assembling or dispersing. Both aims can, according to circumstances, be equally relevant.

The strong emphasis on the problems of *assembling* in the following, therefore, does not mean that assembling ought to be attempted in all circumstances. On the contrary, in many cases good arguments exist for not doing so; for example, to ensure a more even distribution of city activities over larger sections of the city, or to establish peaceful, quiet spaces as supplements to the more lively ones. The extreme concentrations of high-rise towers, functions, and people, as found in many large cities, exemplify what is in many respects a disadvantageous concentration. Less could certainly do.

Emphasis is nevertheless placed on the problems of assembling, partly because it is usually far more difficult to assemble events than to disperse them, and partly because developmental trends in society and planning dogma have established a strong general tendency toward the dispersal of people and events in both new and old urban areas.

assembling people
and events

It is of prime importance to recognize that it is not buildings, but people and events, that need to be assembled. Concepts like floor area/site ratio and building density say nothing conclusive about whether human activities are adequately concentrated.

81

to assemble or disperse

If people and events are assembled sensibly, the result will usually be improved conditions for communal activities as well as for privacy. On one side of the dwelling is a street − on the other side there will be room for a veritable forest. (Siedlung Halen, Bern, Switzerland.)

The design of buildings in relation to relevant human dimensions is crucial – how much can be reached on foot from a given point, and how much it is possible to see and experience. The "dense-low" building project with a great number of houses placed around an intricate path system does not automatically represent a noteworthy concentration of activity, even where building density is high.

Conversely, the village street with its two unbroken rows of houses oriented toward the street represents a clear and consistent assembly of activities. The placement of the buildings and the orientation of the entrances in relation to the pedestrian routes and areas for outdoor stays are the determining factors in this connection.

The fact that the usual radius of action for most people on foot is limited to 400 to 500 meters (1,300 to 1,600 ft.) per excursion [6] and the fact that the possibilities for seeing other people and courses of events are limited to a distance of between 20 and 100 meters (65 and 330 ft.), depending on what is to be seen, in practice place very great demands on the degree of concentration.

If it is to be possible to see other people and events from the home or on a short walk of a little more than a half kilometer (1,600 ft.) and possible to reach the most important services on foot, the activities and functions must necessarily be assembled very carefully. Only a few space-demanding, trivial functions or a slightly excessive distance is needed to turn richness of experience into poverty.

It is, quite simply, of utmost necessity to be very careful with every single foot of facade or pedestrian route.

the large, the medium, and the small scale

The problems involved in assembling or dispersing people and activities must be examined in a broad planning context. Decisions at the large scale, in city and regional planning; at the medium scale, in site planning; and at the small scale are inseparably linked. If the prerequisites for reasonably well-functioning and well-used public spaces are not created through decisions at the primary planning level, a basis seldom exists for working at the small scale. This interrelationship is important because in all cases the small scale – the immediate environment – is where the individual person meets and evaluates decisions made at all planning levels. The battle for high quality in cities and building projects must be won at the very small scale, but preparations for successful work at this level must be made on all planning levels.

83

the town that is a square

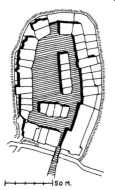

San Vittorino Romano.
Plan 1:4000.

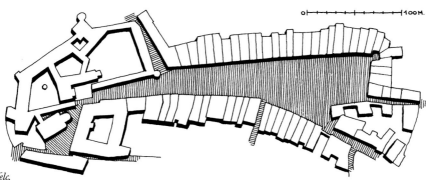

Telc.
Plan 1:4000.

to assemble or
disperse – at the
large scale

At the large scale – in city planning – there is an effective dispersal
of people and events when residences, public services, industries,
and trade functions are placed separately on large individual
tracts of land in a functionally segregated city structure that is
dependent on the automobile as the means of transportation
between units. Dispersal of events and people is a phenomenon
common to nearly all suburban areas worldwide, and in the
sprawling city of Los Angeles it attains its most consistent and
disturbing form.

In contrast to this is the city structure that consistently
assembles events and people in a clear pattern, in which the
public spaces are the most important elements in the city plan,
and where all other functions are effectively located alongside
and facing the streets. Such city structures can be found in
nearly all old cities, and are, in most recent years, again gaining
a foothold in new projects in European cities. The most recent
Swedish new town, Skarpnäck [46], south of Stockholm (see
page 90), is one among several examples of this most interesting
development, where streets and squares have again become the
major elements around which all other functions are located.

to assemble or
disperse – at the
medium scale

At the medium scale – in site planning – people and activities are
dispersed when buildings are placed at great distances from one
another, with entrance areas and residences oriented away from
each other. The pattern is common in traditional single-family
housing areas and functionalistic detached apartment blocks. In
both of these cases a maximum of sidewalk and path connections
occur, with overdimensioned open areas and a consequent
thinning out of outdoor activities.

Conversely, people and activities can be assembled by placing
the individual buildings and functions so that the system of public
spaces is as compact as possible and so that the distances for
pedestrian traffic and sensory experiences are as short as possible.
This principle can be found in nearly all pre-1930 areas and in a
growing number of more recent building projects. In its simplest
and most well-arranged form it can be found also in small towns
where all the buildings are assembled around a square.

San Vittorino Romano, just east of Rome, and the town of Telc
in Czechoslovakia are early examples of this building form. Modern parallels include recent cluster housing projects and a number
of recent Scandinavian cohousing projects.

This organizational principle can be traced throughout history,
from traditional tribal camps to contemporary campsites.

the town that is a street

The town that is a street
(Arnis, northern Germany.)

The town that is a street. All units
placed along a glass covered street.
(Gårdsåkra, Eslöv, Sweden. 1980-
82. Architect Peter Broberg.)

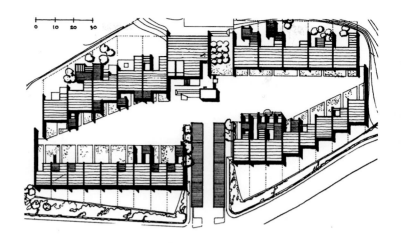

The emphasis on communal living is reflected in the housing layout. Co-op housing Sættedammen, north of Copenhagen (1970). [48]. Plan 1:2000. (Architects T. Bjerg and P. Dyreborg)

The buildings, entrances, tents, and so on are assembled around a public space and turn toward one another like friends around a table.

Building projects oriented around a square are characterized by having a limited number of inhabitants. If the population becomes too large, there is not enough room for everyone around the square – if the square is to retain dimensions that permit the visual assembly of activities.

the town that is a street

In this situation the street lined with low buildings becomes the natural organizational form as a logical consequence of the limitations of human movement and a frontally and horizontally oriented sensory system. When activities are assembled along a street, the individual is able, merely by taking a short walk, to establish what is going on in the area.

This building principle is found in its simplest form in towns built up around a single street. Traditional villages, which developed along a main street, have been mentioned already. A recent example of a town built according to this principle is Gårdsåkra in Eslov, Sweden, designed by the architect Peter Broberg [13]. In Gårdsåkra all the residences, the entrances, the school, the public buildings, and the integrated workshops and offices are assembled along a street. The principle of creating a linear structure has made it possible in this case for the street to be roofed with glass to assure climate protection year-round. The concise, street-oriented site structure has also been used in recent Scandinavian housing areas, where the "town" becomes a street with houses along it.

cities with streets and squares: Skarpnäck, Stockholm

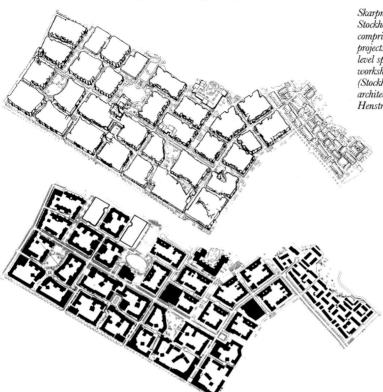

Skarpnäck, a new town south of Stockholm, Sweden (built 1982-88), comprises private and public housing projects for 10,000 inhabitants. Street-level spaces are allocated to offices, workshops, and communal facilities. (Stockholm City Planning Office, architects Leif Blomquist and Eva Henström)

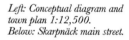

Left: Conceptual diagram and town plan 1:12,500.
Below: Skarpnäck main street.

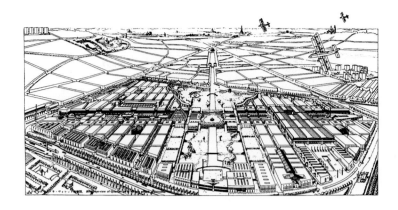

A definite trend away from loose suburbs and toward tight urban patterns of cities with streets and squares is clearly distinguishable in contemporary European planning policies.
(Competition project for La Villette, Paris, 1976. Architect Leon Krier [30].)

cities with streets and squares

Large building projects need more streets and squares with a more differentiated structure that includes main streets, side streets, and primary and secondary squares, such as are found in old cities.

The principle is occasionally found in suburban areas and functionalistic building projects. Generally, however, it is in such a diluted and spread-out fashion that the "streets" have become roads and the "squares" have become huge, open, nondescript areas devoid of people. In this way the individual activities have been dispersed in time and space because of overdimensioning and an unnecessary doubling and spreading of the access roads. It is not the lack of pedestrian traffic and residents that has prevented the establishment of more intimate and better-used public spaces, but rather the decision to have many dispersed roads and paths instead of a more concentrated street network such as that found in the old cities.

In the entire history of human settlement, streets and squares have been the basic elements around which all cities were organized. History has proved the virtues of these elements to such a degree that, for most people, streets and squares constitute the very essence of the phenomenon "city." This simple relationship and the logical use of streets and squares – streets based on the linear pattern of human movement and squares based on the eye's ability to survey an area – have in recent years again been taken up. Leon Krier's projects and theoretical studies [29, 30, 31], Rob Krier's new city areas in Berlin [34], Almere New Town in Holland, and Scandinavian new towns such as Skatudden in Helsinki and Skarpnäck New Town near Stockholm [46] point to an interesting renaissance of the proven principles of cities built around streets and squares.

to assemble or disperse – spatially

In general, the size of spaces in old cities correlates well with the human sensory apparatus and the number of people who use the spaces.
In more recently built communities, an equally careful handling of the spatial dimensions is indeed rare. Nevertheless, a number of exceptions from this general rule can be found.

Top left: Marken, Holland.

Left: Access street 4 meters (12 feet) wide in a recent housing project in Copenhagen.
A width of 4 meters permits a pedestrian flow of 50 to 60 persons per minute. More space is seldom needed!

Below: Suburban street 24 meters (72 feet) wide in Toronto, Ontario. The space creates a seemingly unbridgeable void between the houses.

to assemble or disperse – at the small scale

At the small scale – in the design of the outdoor spaces and adjacent facades – it is necessary to work with detailed and careful planning of the elements that generate and support life between buildings. Individual functions and activities should be evaluated on a case-by-case basis and allotted street frontage in accordance with their value as attractions and their importance for the functioning of the outdoor space. Based on the individual person's limited radius of action and modest sensory range, the design of each foot of street or facade and each square foot of space is of utmost importance.

to assemble or disperse – spatially

At the small scale dispersing activities spatially can be achieved by overdimensioning areas for few people and few activities. Twenty-, thirty-, and forty-meter-wide (65-, 100-, and 135-ft.) pedestrian streets, or squares with a length and width ranging from forty or fifty to sixty meters (135 or 170 to 205 ft.), in residential building projects of modest size, are examples of this. Not only is there a long distance between people from one side to the other in such spaces, but the possibility for those walking through of experiencing simultaneously what is going on at both sides is more or less lost.

Conversely, an attempt can be made to assemble events by dimensioning both streets and squares realistically in relation to the range of the senses and the number of people that can be expected to use the spaces.

Street market, Singapore. Throughout the world the distance between market stalls is from 2 to 3 meters (6 to 9 feet).

The usual distance between stalls in the marketplace and in department stores is 2 to 3 meters (6 to 9 ft.), a size that permits pedestrian traffic, trade on both sides, and a clear view of the merchandise on both sides. In Venice the average street width is a good 3 meters (9 ft.), a dimension that provides room for a pedestrian traffic flow of forty to fifty pedestrians per minute.

That the intensity of experience also is increased with reduced size often will be an additional incentive to careful dimensioning of spaces. It is nearly always more interesting to be in small spaces, where both the whole and the details can be seen – one has the best of both worlds.

Venice and other places with very narrow streets should not necessarily be used as direct models for new streets, but they serve to underline the fact that so many spaces in our modern cities are grossly oversized. It is as if planners and architects have a strong tendency, whenever in doubt, to throw in some extra space, just in case, reflecting the general uncertainty concerning the proper handling of small dimensions and small spaces. *Whenever in doubt, leave some space out.*

small spaces in large
ones

In northern European countries, the climate presents difficult problems with regard to dimensioning outdoor spaces. Small spaces with tall buildings also mean dark and sunless spaces. In southern Europe, it is reasonable and comfortable to have shade and subdued light, but in the north, both light and sun are highly valued qualities. The wish for light and sun, plus a modest-sized space in which people can congregrate, can, however, be combined. The terracing of buildings is one possibility; another is building up small spaces within the large ones. Street spaces with rows of trees demonstrate the value of the principle of small spaces within large ones. Comparably, front yards in front of rowhouses assure both wide, sun-filled spaces and a reasonably narrow, intimate street.

A small space in a large one.

*Above: Rows of trees introduce an intimate scale in the open landscape.
Right: In the wide street space of the Rambla in Bracelona trees and pavilions create an attractive pedestrian space*

to assemble or disperse – along the facade	The design of facades or adjacent areas also provides possibilities for influencing the concentration of activities and the intensity of experience for those who pass by on the sidewalk. The concentration of activities depends on active and closely spaced exchange zones between street and facade and on short distances between entrances and other functions, which contribute to activating the public environment.

Big buildings with long facades, few entrances, and few visitors mean an effective dispersal of events. The principle, in contrast, should be narrow units and many doors.

to assemble or disperse along the facade – in city streets	If activities are to be assembled rather than dispersed in city streets, only the entrances to large buildings, businesses, banks, and offices naturally belong on the facade fronting the public area.

Street life is drastically reduced when small, active units are superseded by large units. In many places it is possible to see how life in the streets has dwindled drastically as gas stations, car dealerships, and parking lots have created holes and voids in the city fabric, or when passive units such as offices and banks move in.

In contrast, examples exist of careful planning in which holes and voids are not accepted, where large units are situated behind or above the small units along the facade. Only the entrances to all functions and the most interesting activities take up space in the facade. This principle is demonstrated in movie theaters, for example, where only the entrance with the ticket

Narrow units and many doors are important principles for concentrating events.
(Java Island, Amsterdam, the Netherlands.)

to assemble or disperse – along the facade

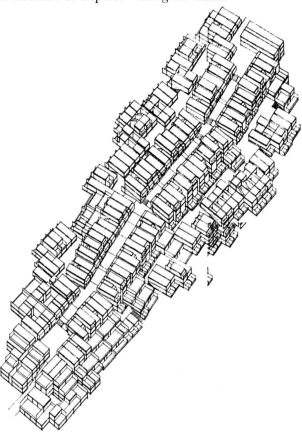

When buildings are narrow, the street length is shortened, the walking distances are reduced, and street life is enhanced.
(Competition project for the extension of Rørås, Norway.)

Narrow street frontages mean short distances between entrances – and entrances are where the majority of events nearly always take place.

booth and advertising are placed on the street, while the auditorium itself is well hidden somewhere behind. This should be the standard solution when banks and offices must be located on city streets.

To counteract the problem of the dull and dying facades, many Danish cities have passed building codes to restrict the establishment of banks and offices at street level. Other Danish cities very successfully have allowed banks and offices to be established on city streets, but only as long as the street frontage is not in excess of five meters (15 ft.).

Not surprisingly, the practice of giving each unit the shortest possible street facade is found in all new suburban shopping malls. Knowing that pedestrians generally do not wish to walk very far, shopping mall designers logically use narrow frontages, so that there is room for as many shops as possible in the shortest possible street distance.

Using the principle of narrow, deep lots along with the careful use of frontage space avoids the problems of "holes" and "left-over-areas" wherever buildings face sidewalks and pedestrian routes. This is also true in residential areas. Good examples of such site plans are found in many traditional rowhouse projects and in a number of building projects, such as Siedlung Halen in Bern, Switzerland (see illustration on page 84) and more recent residential areas on Java, Borneo, and Sporenburg Islands in the Harbor of Amsterdam.

In city streets, the length of frontages should be carefully dimensioned.
A rhythm frequently found in shopping streets in all parts of the world is 15-25 units per 100 meters.
(Street from the old town in Stockholm, Sweden.)

to assemble on one level – or disperse over several levels

City center in Coventry, England.
Pedestrians tend to use the ground
level only.

In streets with low buildings,
everything is visible as far as the
eye can reach.
In high-rise building areas, only
the ground-floor level is within the
field of vision.

to assemble on one level – or disperse over several levels

In addition to the already mentioned options for dispersing or assembling events, the possibility of assembling or dispersing on one or more levels also exists.

The problem is very simple. Activities that take place on the same level can be experienced within the range limitation of the senses, that is, within a radius of from 20 to 100 meters (65 to 330 ft.), depending on what is to be seen, and in this situation it is easy to move about among activities. If something happens on a level that is only a short distance up, possibilities for experiences are greatly reduced. Crawling up a tree always has been a good way of hiding.

The problem is less pronounced when something occurs on a lower level – one can often have a fine overview from the higher position – but participation and interaction are still physically and psychologically difficult. The effect with regard to use of the elevated public spaces is clearly seen in William H. Whyte's studies from New York City [51]. "Sight lines are important. If people do not see a space, they will not use it." And with regard to sunken spaces, he writes, "Unless there is a compelling reason, an open space should never be sunk. With two or three notable exceptions, sunken plazas are dead spaces."

Dispersal over several levels.
(Street scene, Los Angeles.)

to assemble on one level – or disperse over several levels

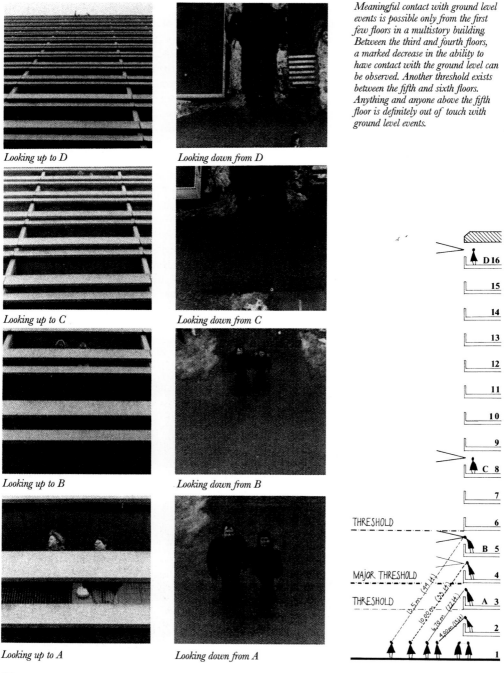

Looking up to D

Looking down from D

Looking up to C

Looking down from C

Looking up to B

Looking down from B

Looking up to A

Looking down from A

Meaningful contact with ground level events is possible only from the first few floors in a multistory building. Between the third and fourth floors, a marked decrease in the ability to have contact with the ground level can be observed. Another threshold exists between the fifth and sixth floors. Anything and anyone above the fifth floor is definitely out of touch with ground level events.

D 16
15
14
13
12
11
10
9
C 8
7
THRESHOLD 6
B 5
MAJOR THRESHOLD 4
THRESHOLD A 3
2
1

In principle, therefore, it is a bad idea to attempt to assemble activities by placing them above one another on different levels. Lookout points can be placed high up, but not activities that one wishes to assemble. If this is attempted regardless, the result is often disappointing because functions located 50 to 100 meters (170 to 330 ft.) from one another along a street interrelate more readily than functions placed just 3 meters (10 ft.) over or 3 meters (10 ft.) under one another.

These experiences can be transferred meaningfully to the discussion of low versus tall buildings. Low buildings along a street are in harmony with the way in which people move about and the way in which the senses function, as opposed to tall buildings, which are not.

Low buildings along a street are in harmony with the way in which people move about and the way the senses function. Tall buildings are not. (Street scene, Singapore).

to assemble on one level or disperse over several levels – "underground cities" and "skywalks"

The undesirable dispersal of people and events that takes place when there are many parallel paths instead of a compact street system has already been discussed. A comparable form of undesirable dispersal is found when comprehensive underground pedestrian networks or various forms of "skywalks" are established, and access routes are layered above one another. Skywalks, found in city centers as well as in residential areas, are, as a rule, a questionable idea in both situations.

If an assembling of events and people is desired, a better solution is found in, for example, the three-story residential areas in Montreal in Canada. All activities and residents are led by balconies and stairs down to one level. In addition, a living, inspiring street facade is created, as well as good opportunities for outdoor stays directly in front of the individual homes.

Skywalks and balcony access disperse people and events, while access stairs bring the inhabitants together, in the streets.
Above: Housing scheme, Edinburgh, Scotland.
Below: Residential area, Montreal. Quebec.

To Integrate or Segregate

 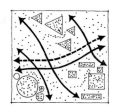

a differentiated
contact "surface"

Integration implies that various activities and categories of people are permitted to function together or side by side. Segregation implies a separation of functions and groups that differ from one another.

Integration of various activities and functions in and around public spaces allows the people involved to function together and to stimulate and inspire one another. In addition, the mixing of various functions and people makes it possible to interpret how the surrounding society is composed and how it operates.

With regard to this issue as well, it is not the formal integration of buildings and primary city functions but the actual integration of various events and people on the very small scale that determines whether the contact surface is monotonous or interesting. What is important is not whether factories, residences, service functions, and so on are placed close together on the architects' drawings, but whether the people who work and live in the different buildings use the same public spaces and meet in connection with daily activities.

planning models for
integration and
segregation

The development from the compact medieval city with a close, interwoven pattern of activities to the highly specialized, functionalistic city illustrates the possibilities for mixing and separating people and events in connection with physical planning.

In the old medieval cities, pedestrian traffic dictated a city structure in which merchants and craftsmen, rich and poor, young and old, necessarily had to live and work side by side. Such cities embody the advantages and disadvantages of an integration-oriented city structure.

Comparably, segregation-oriented planning is illustrated by functionalistic city structure, in which separation of unlike functions was the goal. The result was a city divided into monofunctional areas.

101

The large, unbroken residential area with uniform residential groups, the dull and monotonous industrial areas, and the large, identical pseudo-cities built up around a single function or group of people, such as the research complex, university town, and retirement village, are all examples of such monofunctional areas.

In these areas a single group of people, a single occupation, a single social group or age group has been more or less isolated from the other groups in society.

The benefit perhaps has been a more rational planning process, shorter distance between similar functions, and greater efficiency, but the price has been reduced contact with the surrounding society, a poorer and more monotonous environment.

An alternative to these planning models is a more differentiated planning policy, in which social relations and practical advantages are evaluated from function to function and in which separation is only accepted when the disadvantages of assembling clearly outweigh the advantages. For example, only a very small group of the most annoying industrial activities is unsuitable for integration with residences.

to integrate
– at the large scale

At the large scale a consistent effort can be made to mix all functions that do not oppose or interfere with one another.

An integration-oriented city plan can do this by describing growth directions or areas to be extended at various *times*, rather than by various *functions*, specifying growth segments for the years 2005 to 2010 to 2015 instead of residential, industrial, and public service areas.

the city that is a
university
– and vice versa

An integration-oriented city plan can also be one in which large functions are used as an opportunity to fit many small units into a wider context. Urban plans can, for example, use a new university as an obvious occasion to place a sizable number of residences and businesses in an integrated city structure – a university city with residences and businesses. That old, integrated city structures still exist side by side with new, monofunctional areas makes it possible to study both planning principles.

The University of Copenhagen is predominantly placed in the center of the old city. The main building is situated centrally, and spread out around it in the city are schools, colleges, and departments in a number of different locations that were found as space became needed. The streets of the city are part of the university and function both as internal and external connecting corridors.

Without doubt the scattering of the university throughout the city causes a number of disadvantages to the institution as an administrative unit. But for those involved, the near contact with the city creates innumerable possibilities for using the city and participating in its life. And for the city the placement of the university means a valuable contribution of energy, life, and activities.

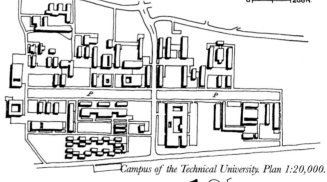

The campus of the Technical University, Copenhagen. Organized around the central parking lot.

0 ———— 200 M.

Campus of the Technical University. Plan 1:20,000.

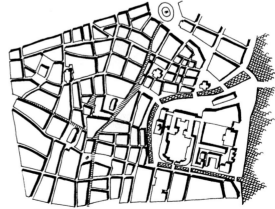

For comparison, the entire inner-city area of Copenhagen. Plan 1:20,000.

The counterpart is the "rationally" planned institute of higher education – a university campus – such as the campus of the Technical University of Denmark outside Copenhagen. Under this plan education is systematized, and connecting routes from department to department are rationally organized; on the other hand, "the city" contains very little activity. There is no basis for many resulting activities. There are only few cafeterias and newsstands, and all who use the area constitute only one category of people: students and faculty.

The education of one-sided, overspecialized technicians is nurtured under the best possible conditions – a one-sided, overspecialized environment – as the direct daily connection between the study environment and the society in general has been severed.

Three city functions that together could have formed the basis for a lively city, if the planning concept had been to create cities instead of isolated, monofunctional areas.
Upper left: A high rise housing area with 7,000 inhabitants, surrounded by parking lots and lawns.
Below left: The Danish national broadcasting and television complex. Fifteen hundred people, surrounded by parking lots and uninhabited green lawns, work here on the production and administration of television programs.
Below right: School and teacher training college with 1,500 students, in similar isolation.

integration – at the small scale

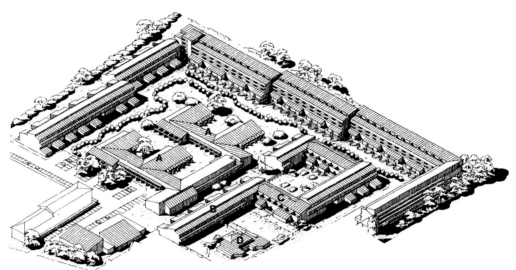

Above: Integrating young and old
age groups in a new housing area.
Four hundred apartments and
maisonettes surrounding home and
service center for the elderly (A),
day-care center, kindergarten, and
youth facilities (B, C, and D).
(Solbjerg Have, urban renewal area
in Copenhagen, 1978-81.
Architects: Fællestegnestuen)

106

The rejection of monofunctional areas is a prerequisite for the integration of various types of people and activities. If the possibilities are to be redeemed, planning and design work at the medium and the very small scale are decisive factors.

For example, schools can be located in the middle of a housing development and still be effectively separated from the surroundings – by fences, walls, and lawns. But schools can also be designed as an integral part of housing. Classrooms, for example, can be placed around the city's public streets, which then serve as corridors and playgrounds. The café on the square doubles as the school's cafeteria, and the city thus becomes a part of the educational process. Commercial and other city functions can be located similarly along the street or in the public area itself, so that the borders between different functions and groups of people are removed. Each activity is given a chance to work with another.

The architect F. van Klingeren's city centers in Dronten and Eindhoven in Holland [11] illustrate this planning principle and its possibilities.

The city center has become a covered square, provided with sports equipment, movie screens, spectator stands, chairs, and so on, so that it can be used in a multitude of ways. In principle the square functions exactly like a traditional square.
Trade, football, political meetings, religious services, concerts, theater, performances, sidewalk cafés, exhibitions, play, and dance can coexist in the square. The ensuing result has been a much higher level of overall participation of the townspeople in the various activities than is customary in other comparable Dutch towns.

Integration has also been the key word in many improvement projects in monotonous multistory residential areas built during the 1960s.
In such a renewal project in Sweden, several former apartment buildings have been renovated to house light industry, offices, and residences for the elderly, to give the area greater diversity.

This integration policy has achieved remarkably positive results.

The example of the private living room in the home can serve as a model for integration of activities on any other scale. In the living room all members of the family can be occupied with various activities at the same time, but individual activities and people can also function together.

107

to integrate or segregate traffic

Above: Separating various traffic modes results in boring path and road systems.
Below: When all traffic is on foot, as in Venice, the separation of traffic from other city activities never becomes an issue.

Among all the activities that take place in the public domain, traffic – people and goods on the way from one place to another – is the most comprehensive.

In an ordinary traffic pattern, in mixed streets, where traffic is divided between pedestrians, bicycles and automobiles, a pronounced spreading and separation of people and activities results. When those in transit are further dispersed through a differentiated road system, in which each type of traffic has its own route, the separation is complete. It becomes duller to drive, duller to walk, and duller to live along the roads and streets because a significant number of the people in transit are now segregated from other city activities.

As an alternative to the differentiated street systems, other ways of using cars and the other rapid means of transportation can be envisaged.

For example, greater portions of the individual trips can be transferred from automobile systems to combined networks of public transit, pedestrian, and bicycle systems.

The importance of an integrated transportation system to city life can be observed in those cities in which transportation has always been on foot.

In Europe there are a modest number of old cities in which traffic and city life have never been split up into motor and pedestrian traffic. This is true of a number of hill towns in Italy, the stairway cities in Yugoslavia, the Greek island cities, and Venice, which has a special place among pedestrian cities, both because it is by far the largest, with over 250,000 inhabitants, and because it is the most thoroughly worked-out and refined example of this type of city.

In Venice the heavy goods transport takes place on the canals, while the pedestrian system still functions as the city's primary traffic network.

Here life and traffic exist side by side in the same space, which functions simultaneously as a space for outdoor stays and a connecting link. In this context traffic presents no security problems, no exhaust fumes, noise, and dirt, and therefore it has never been necessary to separate work, rest, meals, play, entertainment, and transit.

Venice is a living room with integrated processes enlarged to city scale.

This same concept explains the civilized Venetian practice of arriving late at prearranged meetings, because people inevitably meet friends and acquaintances or stop to look at something while walking through the city.

four traffic planning principles

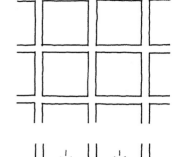

Los Angeles

Traffic integration on the terms of the fast-moving traffic. A straightforward, simple traffic system with a low degree of traffic safety. The streets are unusable for anything but vehicular traffic.

Radburn

Traffic separation system introduced in 1928 in Radburn, New Jersey: a complicated, expensive system involving many parallel roads and paths and many costly underpasses. Surveys of residential districts show that this principle, which in theory appears to improve traffic safety, functions poorly in practice because pedestrians follow shorter routes rather than safer, more lengthy, routes.

Delft

Traffic integration on the terms of slow-moving traffic. Introduced in 1969, the system is simple, straightforward, and safe, maintaining the street as the all-important public space.
When cars must be driven up to a building, this system of integration is by far superior to the two systems above.

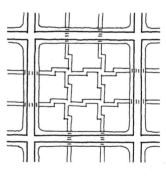

Venice

The pedestrian city. Transition from fast to slow-moving traffic on the outskirts of the city or the area. A straightforward and simple traffic system with a considerably higher safety level and greater feeling of security than any other system.

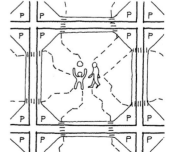

transfer to slow traffic
at the city limits

The main traffic principle in Venice is that a transfer from fast to slow traffic occurs at the city limits and not at the front door, as has become customary through the years in most places where the automobile has come into use.

The principle of leaving cars at the city limits or at the edge of residential areas and walking the last 50 to 100 to 150 meters (170 to 330 to 500 ft.) home through the neighborhood has in recent times become widespread in European residential areas. This is a positive development that permits local traffic to become integrated again with other outdoor activities.

integration of local
traffic on pedestrian
terms

The effort to integrate local automobile traffic on pedestrian terms is also a positive development. This principle was first introduced in Holland, where local areas have been designed or renovated for slow automobile traffic.

In these *Woonerf* areas, automobiles are permitted to drive right up to the front doors but the streets are clearly designed as pedestrian areas, in which cars are forced to proceed at low speeds between the established staying and play areas. Cars are guests in the pedestrians' domain.

The concept of integrating automobile traffic on pedestrian terms offers considerable advantages over methods that segregate traffic. Even though completely car-free areas have both a higher degree of traffic security and a better design and dimensioning for outdoor stays and pedestrian traffic and so offer an optimal solution, the Dutch concept of traffic integration in many cases offers a very acceptable alternative, the second-best solution.

integration of traffic
and outdoor stays

Regardless of whether residential areas are built according to the Venetian principle, with a transfer from rapid to slow traffic at the city limits, or according to the Dutch *Woonerf* principle, with multifunctional streets for slow automobile as well as bicycle and pedestrian traffic, it is important that efforts be made to integrate traffic and activities related to outdoor stays. When traffic consists of pedestrians or of cars moving at slow speeds, the arguments for separating staying and play areas from the areas for traffic lose their validity. The fact that traffic to and from houses in nearly all instances is the most comprehensive of all outdoor activities in residential areas is good reason for seeking to integrate as many other activities as possible with the traffic. For those in transit, for children at play, and for those involved with activities around the houses, a policy

111

Where cars must be driven right up to building entrances, the best solution is the Dutch "Woonerf" principle, in which streets accommodate slow-moving traffic, pedestrians, and bicycles. The streets are detailed in a way that clearly indicates their status as predominantly "soft traffic" areas. Traffic speed is further reduced by low ramps and other restraints. Right: Dutch street before and after conversion to "Woonerf" street.

of traffic integration will enable different activities to support and stimulate one another.

Many activities – play, outdoor stays, conversations – get started when one is actually involved with something else or on the way somewhere.

Outdoor stays and transit are not finite, sharply demarcated activities. Their limits are flexible; the same people are involved in both.

Different categories of activities have a strong tendency to weave themselves together – if they are allowed to do so.

To Invite or Repel

 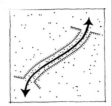

to invite or repel

Public spaces in the city and in residential areas can be inviting and easily accessible and thus encourage people and activities to move from the private to the public environment. Conversely, public spaces can be designed so that it is difficult to get out into them, physically and psychologically.

invitation – smooth transitions between public and private areas

Whether the public environment invites or repels is, among other things, a question of how the public environment is placed in relation to the private, and how the border zone between the two areas is designed. Sharply demarcated borders – such as those found in multistory residences, where one is either in a completely private territory indoors and upstairs or in a completely public area outside on the stairs, in the elevator, or on the street – will make it difficult in many situations to move into the public environment if it is not necessary to do so.

Flexible boundaries in the form of transitional zones that are neither completely private nor completely public, on the other hand, will often be able to function as connecting links, making it easier, both physically and psychologically, for residents and activities to move back and forth between private and public spaces, between in and out. This very important issue is examined in more detail in a following section (see page 185).

invitation – to be able to see what is going on

Being able to see what is going on in public spaces also can be an element of invitation.

If children can see the street or playground from their homes, they also can follow what is happening and see who is outside playing. They then are more often motivated to go out and play, in contrast to the children who cannot see what is going on because they live too high up or too far away.

Numerous examples that emphasize the relationship between being able to see and the desire to participate can likewise be found among adult activities. Youth clubs and community

invitation – gradual transition from indoors to out

A gradual transition between public and private spaces greatly assists people in participating in or keeping in close contact with life and events in the public space.

Top: Semiprivate front yards in rowhouse area.
Right: Gradual transitional zones in a multistory residence – but only for the ground floor. (Almere, The Netherlands)
The street as invitation. (Saint Paul Baie, Quebec)

centers with windows on the street have more members than clubs in basement rooms because passersby are inspired to join in by seeing what is going on and who is participating. Merchants, incidentally, have always known that it is all-important to be located precisely where people pass by and to have display windows facing the street. In much the same way, the sidewalk café works as a direct invitation to join in.

invitation – a short
and manageable route

An invitation can also be a question of a short and manageable route between the private and the public environment. Many examples illustrate the great influence of factors such as distance, route quality, and mode of transportation on the connections between people and between various functions.

Small children seldom move more than 50 meters (170 ft.) from their front doors, and even within this small radius distance seems to play a part. Children play more often with a neighbor's children than with children who live just a little farther away.

It is also common that family and friends who live near one another see one another more than they see acquaintances who live farther away. Informal contact situations such as "dropping in" play a larger part when the people involved live close by. This again can have a positive influence on other contact forms.

Public libraries, too, have noted a direct relationship between distance and book borrowing. Those who live nearest to the library and who can get there most easily also borrow the most books.

motivation shifting
– excursions as
excuses

Among the requirements that are satisfied, in part, in public spaces are the need for contact, the need for knowledge, and the need for stimulation. These belong to the group of psychological needs. Satisfying these is seldom as goal-oriented and deliberate as with the more basic physical needs, such as eating, drinking, sleeping, and so on. For example, adults seldom go to town with the expressed intention of satisfying the need for stimulation or the need for contact. Regardless of what the true purpose may be, one goes out for a plausible, rational reason – to shop, to take a walk, to get some fresh air, to buy a paper, to wash the car, and so forth.

Perhaps it is wrong to speak of the shopping excursion as a pretext for contact and stimulation, because very few people out shopping will accept the fact that the need for contact and stimulation plays any part in their shopping plans. The fact that adults who work at home on an average spend nearly three times

Regardless of all the play equipment and fantasy invested in them, playgrounds are fundamentally meeting places. The playground provides a place where children can always go, and the play equipment provides opportunities for passing the time alone until other children arrive and more worthwhile activities can begin.

as much time shopping as those who work outside the home, and the fact that the shopping excursions are distributed evenly throughout the week, even though shopping once a week would perhaps be easier, make it natural to assume that the many daily shopping excursions are not only a question of getting supplies.

It is a general characteristic that basic physical and psychological needs are satisfied at the same time, and that the basic and easily defined needs often serve to explain and motivate the satisfying of both sets of needs. In this context the shopping excursion is both a shopping trip and a pretext, or occasion, for contact and stimulation.

invitation
– somewhere to go

This interweaving of motives emphasizes the importance of destinations in the public environment: things and places that the individual can seek out naturally and use as a motive and inducement to go out. Destinations can be outings to particular places, lookout points, places to watch the sun set, or they can be shops, community centers, sports facilities, and so forth.

In a village society, with a communal well and washhouse, it may still be possible to see these two facilities function as the all-dominant catalysts for informal contact situations. The pretexts are perhaps even systematized, as in San Vittorino Romano (see page 86), where traditionally pails were left at the well so it was always possible to "go out and get the pail" if somebody to talk to turned up.

In southern Europe the bars also play an important role as destinations. One goes to the bar for a glass of wine, but one also is sure of meeting friends. In other parts of the world, pubs, drugstores, and cafés serve the same purpose as destinations and pretexts.

In new residential areas, mailboxes, newsstands, restaurants, shops, and sports facilities must assume the role of acceptable pretexts for the individual to be in and stay in the public environment.

For children, the playground is the place where one can always go. This role, in fact, is one of the playground's most important functions. Even though most playgrounds have only limited uses, and children play in places other than the playground during most of their time outdoors, the playground has an important function as a meeting place, as a starting place for other children's activities.

Whether or not others are outside playing, children can always go to the playground, and there is always something to do – as a start.

invitation – something to do

Something to do.
Left: Minigarden in English multistory housing area.

Below: Lane maintenance day in a Danish residential area.
All generations are involved, and a neighborhood party often crowns the day of group activity.

In the same way that children use the playground as a place to go to and use the play equipment there until other things can get started, gardens and gardening, for example, can serve the same purposes quite well for other age groups.

When the weather is good and it is pleasant to be outdoors for a while, the garden provides meaningful activity, something to do. If the garden is located where people pass by or where there is a good view of other activities, work in the garden is often combined with other, recreational and social activities. The useful is combined with the pleasurable.

A closer study of front yard activities [21] shows that in many instances there are such subtle combinations of purposes and that gardening serves as a pretext for being outdoors. It can be noted that many people – not least the oldest residents – spend

If there is something to do, there may also be something to talk about afterward. Necessary, optional, and social activities are interwoven in countless subtle ways.

considerably more time on gardening than can be justified in any way for strictly horticultural purposes.

This emphasizes how important it is that in public spaces in residential areas there are not only opportunities for walking and sitting, but also opportunities to act, things to do, activities to be involved in. This should be supplemented preferably with possibilities for taking small, daily domestic activities, such as potato peeling, sewing, repair jobs, hobbies, and meals, out into the public spaces.

If facilities are provided for bringing ordinary domestic activities – repairs, hobbies, meal preparations, and meals – out on the public side of the residences, life between buildings can be substantially enriched. (Top: North Toronto. Below: Brooklyn, New York.)

To Open Up or Close In

 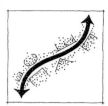

to open up or close in

Contact through experience between what is taking place in the public environment and what is taking place in the adjacent residences, shops, factories, workshops, and communal buildings can provide a marked extension and enrichment of possibilities for experiences, in both directions.

To open up for a two-way exchange of experiences is not only a question of glass and windows but also a question of distances. The narrow parameters of human sensory experiences play a part in determining whether an event is opened up or closed in.

The library with large windows, with a 10- to 15-meter (33- to 50-ft.) setback, and the library with windows directly on the street illustrate the two situations. In one case it is possible to see a building with windows; in the other, a library in use.

a common planning policy

It is remarkable how few events and functions in new building and urban renewal projects are made visually accessible.

Many activities are closed in, apparently without any obvious motive other than because a swimming pool, a youth center, a bowling alley, or a waiting room is usually closed in.

In other instances considerations of efficiency appear to have played an important part. Schoolchildren are not able to look out of the windows, and may not be seen, in order not to be disturbed. Factory workers must, with regard to productivity, manage with fluorescent lighting and carefully monitored public address system music. Office workers in a high-rise building may look out at the clouds but not at the street, and so on. Only where openness and accessibility may directly assist in promoting commerce is the view opened up to merchandise and, if necessary, human activities.

an alternative planning policy

Both the unthinking and the conscious fencing in of people and activities is questionable in most cases. Instead, a planning

to open up or close in

Left: Although this shop is open seven days a week, it is certainly not open towards the sidewalk at any time. (Adelaide, Australia.)

Below: An exciting contribution to the street environment: glass between the pavement and a swimming pool. (Vesterbro, Copenhagen, Denmark.)

to open up or close in – in residential areas

*»My home is my castle«
can be taken far too literally.*

*Right: In new Scandinavian
residential areas great efforts
are made to open up the residences and extend the sphere of
influence and surveillance well
into the access streets by way
of balconies, frontyards and
glassed-in verandas.
(Sibeliusparken, 1984-86,
Copenhagen. Architects:
Fællestegnestuen.)*

policy that is based on a case-by-case evaluation of individual
situations and the advantages and disadvantages for those involved can be suggested. Often it will be natural to differentiate
subtly between the open and the closed.

It might be advantageous to be able to see from a retirement
residence or hospital the activities taking place in public spaces,
but the opposite is not true. Some rooms in a nursery school
perhaps should be open toward the street, but not others; the
public swimming pool or badminton court perhaps should be
placed so far below street level that people who look in through
the windows cannot disturb the activities because the windows
are placed high up, and so forth.

123

"privatizing" public life

A rapidly increasing number of shopping arcades, interior court-yards , plazas, and other seemingly public spaces dilute life in the adjacent public streets and squares. "The Commons" is — as a matter of fact — rather private and rather controlled.

*"The Swiss cheese syndrome. "
A maze of private shopping
arcades crisscrossing the urban
blocks.
(Perth, Western Australia.)*

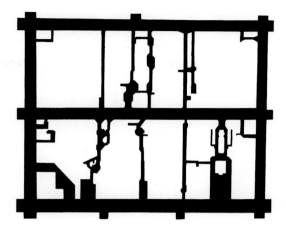

"privatizing" public
life

Recent years have seen a marked tendency to create seemingly public spaces in private buildings, shopping areas, and so on. Private shopping arcades crossing urban blocks, underground street systems, and huge indoor "squares" in hotels are examples.

This trend, seen from a developer's point of view, may create very interesting perspectives, but seen from the point of view of the city, the result will almost always be a dispersal of people and an effective closing in of people and activities, emptying the public spaces of human beings and interesting attractions. The city thus becomes depopulated, duller, and more dangerous, when instead, the same functions, now closed in, could have enhanced many public spaces and the city as a whole.

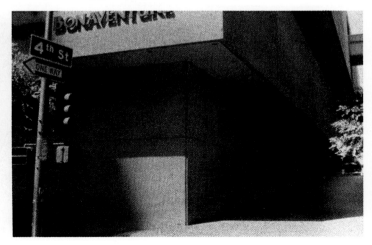

*Inside: A refined interior square catering for selected types of "public life."
Outside: A completely blank wall facing the city. (Hotel complex, Los Angeles.)*

125

making transportation public or private

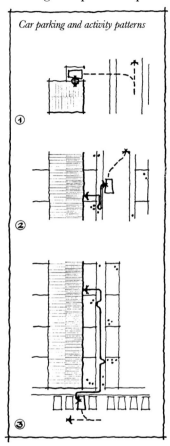

Car parking and activity patterns

①

②

③

If it is deemed necessary to drive private cars right up to the building, activities in the public spaces will generally be substantially reduced.

In residential areas where cars are parked some distance away rather than next to the buildings, the walk through the neighborhood to and from the car constitutes an important and pleasant part of every trip.

1. When cars are parked at the entrance, only cars will be found in the street.

2. When cars are parked at the curb, people as well as cars will be found in the street. Greater opportunities for neighbor contacts will materialize.

3. When cars are parked at the end of the road, pedestrian traffic replaces vehicular traffic.
(From street studies in Melbourne [21].)

With regard to the possibilities for seeing who is on the move and, for those moving about, to see what is going on, the trend from pedestrian to motor traffic has meant a deterioration.

In pedestrian cities people move through their city; in automobile cities only cars are on the streets. People and events are, to be sure, present in cars, but seen from the sidewalk, the picture is both too fragmented and too brief for one to be able to see who is moving and what is going on. The movement of people has become automobile traffic.

The many cars, movements, variations, and the many little glimpses of people can nevertheless have a certain attraction, as evidenced by benches along the streets, spectators at road intersections, and the tendency to prefer walking in streets with automobile traffic to walking on deserted paths. But the pleasure of watching cars is limited and is only observed in situations where there is no more worthwhile offer of experience around. This can be seen, for example, in Italian cities with and without piazzas. If there is a well-functioning piazza, people congregate there, but if there is no piazza and no city life, then street corners at traffic intersections become meeting places, where at least there is something to look at.

The opposite of this situation is again the old pedestrian cities, like Venice, where the offer of experiencing the movement of people and merchandise plays a crucial part in reading and interpreting how the city is put together and how it works. When a bridal couple leaves the church they do not get into a black limousine but continue on foot through the city followed by the wedding guests. When musicians go to work, they walk through the city with their instruments under their arms, and when people dressed in their best are on their way to parties or to the theater, they too are on foot.

Valuable in this context is the trend in recent residential building projects to park cars up to 100 to 200 meters (300 to 660 ft.) from the residences. Streets in these areas are more populated and more entertaining to be in and look at, and chances for frequent, informal meetings of neighbors are increased. That the risk of vandalism and crime is also reduced is yet another positive consequence of traffic being opened up rather than it being enclosed in cars or hidden away on separate road systems or in underground access roads and parking facilities.

4. SPACES FOR WALKING PLACES FOR STAYING: Detail Planning

how often spaces are used is one thing – more important is how they can be used

The preceding sections discuss ways to assemble people and functions in time and space and ways to integrate, invite, and open up rather than close in activities through city and site planning. Thus, primarily the incidence of activities is influenced: that is, *how many* people actually come. But the activity level and number of events do not in themselves describe the quality of the public environment.

That people and events are assembled in time and space is a prerequisite for anything at all to occur, but of more importance is which activities are allowed to develop. It is not enough merely to create spaces that enable people to come and go. Favorable conditions for moving about in and lingering in the spaces must also exist, as well as those for participating in a wide range of social and recreational activities.

In this context the quality of the individual segments of the outdoor environment plays a crucial part. Design of individual spaces and of the details, down to the smallest component, are determining factors.

outdoor activities and outdoor space quality

As discussed earlier in this book, it is important to note how the various categories of outdoor activities are influenced by the quality of outdoor space, and in particular how it is precisely the optional, largely recreational functions and social activities that are given a chance to develop where such quality is improved.

Conversely, it has been noted how these very activities tend to disappear where the quality has been reduced.

In this section, where the subject is not the number of events but the character and content of outdoor life, it is important to note that these activities, which make it particularly attractive and meaningful to be in public spaces, also are the activities that are the most sensitive to the quality of the physical environment.

129

the battle for quality is won or lost at the small scale

Treatment of details is a crucial factor in the usability of outdoor spaces.
When carefully detailed, outdoor spaces stand a good chance of being functional and popular.
If detailing is careless or absent altogether, the battle will inevitably be lost.
Left: Residential area, Milton Keynes, England.
Below: Residential area, Sandvika, Sweden.
(Architect Ralph Erskine)

the battle for quality is won – or lost – at the small scale

Decisions at the city and site planning levels can establish the basis for the creation of well-functioning outdoor spaces. It is, however, only through careful consideration at the detail planning level that the potential possibilities can come into their own. Or, if such work is neglected, the potential can be wasted.

The following section discusses a number of quality demands on the outdoor environment in more detail: some are general demands and some are more specific demands that concern simple, basic activities such as walking, standing, and sitting, as well as seeing, hearing, and talking.

These basic activities are used as a starting point because they are a part of nearly all other activities. If spaces make it attractive to walk, stand, sit, see, hear, and talk, this is in itself an important quality, but it also means that a broad spectrum of other activities – play, sports, community activities, and so on – will have a good basis for development. This is the case partly because many qualities are common to all activities and partly because larger, more complex community activities can develop naturally from the many small daily activities. The big events evolve from the many small ones.

children, adults, and old people

Children's special demands on the outdoor environment are considered along with those of other age groups. The following discussion emphasizes quality demands in general and, additionally, the demands of adults and the elderly on outdoor spaces.

This order of priority is based on an urgent need to examine the outdoor activities and requirements of these groups. Furthermore, support of the outdoor activities of adults and the elderly is in itself considered the best conceivable support for children's activities and the environment in which they grow up.

Walking

walking

Walking is first and foremost a type of transportation, a way to get around, but it also provides an informal and uncomplicated possibility for being present in the public environment. One walks to do an errand, to see the surroundings, or just to walk, all in one process – or in three.

The act of walking is often a necessary act but can also merely be an excuse for being present – "I will just walk by."

Common to all forms of foot traffic are a number of physically and physiologically determined demands on the physical environment.

room to walk

Walking demands space; it is necessary to be able to walk reasonably freely without being disturbed, without being pushed, and without having to maneuver too much. The problem here is to define the human level of tolerance for interferences encountered during walking so that spaces are sufficiently narrow and rich in experiences, yet still wide enough to allow room to maneuver.

Tolerances and demands for space vary a great deal from person to person, within groups of people, and from situation to situation. This relationship is illustrated by observations of the traditional evening stroll in the square at Ioanninna, a city in northern Greece.

At the end of the afternoon, when the stroll begins, the number of participants is small, consisting mainly of parents with children and elderly people who walk up and down the square.

Gradually, as it gets dark and more and more people come out, first the children and then the elderly disappear. Later, as the crowd grows, many middle-aged adults and others withdraw from the bustle. By mid-evening, when the square is the most crowded, practically only the young people of the city continue to stroll back and forth in the throng.

133

In situations where the degree of crowding can be determined freely, the upper limit for an acceptable density in streets and on sidewalks with two-way pedestrian traffic appears to be around 10 to 15 pedestrians per minute per meter ($3^1/_3$ ft.) street width. This corresponds to a pedestrian flow of some one hundred people per minute in a 10-meter-wide (33-ft.) pedestrian street. If the intensity is increased further, a clear tendency toward dividing the pedestrian traffic into two parallel opposite streams is observed.When the pedestrians are consequently required to keep to the right in the street to get through it, freedom of movement is more or less lost. People no longer meet but walk behind one another in ranks. The overcrowding is too great.

If the pedestrian stream is very limited, streets can be comparably narrow. Small streets in the old cities are, like the indoor hallways of the home, seldom wider than 1 meter ($3^1/_3$ ft.), and country footpaths are seldom over 30 centimeters (1 ft.) wide.

Special demands for space are required by the "wheeled" walking traffic: the baby carriage, the wheelchair, the shopping cart, and so forth. Consideration for this traffic will generally necessitate more ample dimensioning than that just described. What space requirements can mean to baby carriage traffic was demonstrated when Strøget, the main street in Copenhagen, was converted from a mixed street with motor traffic and closely packed sidewalks to a walking street with a pedestrian area four times as wide. While the number of pedestrians increased during the first year by approximately 35 percent, the number of baby carriages increased by 400 percent.

paving materials and street surface conditions

Pedestrian traffic is quite sensitive to pavement and surface conditions. Cobblestones, sand, loose gravel, and an uneven ground surface are in most cases unsuitable, especially for those who have walking difficulties.

Adverse surface conditions can also have a negative influence on pedestrian travel in general. People avoid wet and slippery pavements, water, snow, and slush whenever possible. Those with walking problems are particularly inconvenienced under such circumstances.

physical distance versus experienced distance

Acceptable walking distance is a highly subjective matter. The quality of a route is just as important as its actual length.

walking distances
– physical distance,
experienced distance

Walking is physically demanding, and there are narrow limits as to how far most people can or will walk.

In a large number of surveys, the acceptable walking distances for most people in ordinary daily situations has been found to be around 400 to 500 meters (1,300 to 1,600 ft.) [6]. For children, old people, and disabled people, the acceptable walking distance is often considerably less.

Crucial to determining the acceptable distance in a given situation is not only the actual *physical distance*, but also to a great extent the *experienced distance*.

A stretch of 500 meters (1,600 ft.) viewed as a straight, unprotected, and dull path is experienced as very long and tiring, while the same length can be experienced as a very short distance if the route is perceived in stages. For example, the street can wind a bit, so the space is closed and the distance to be walked is not immediately visible, provided that the walk takes place under good external conditions.

Acceptable walking distances thus are an interplay between the length of the street and the quality of the route, both with regard to protection and to stimulation en route.

walking routes

The fact that it is tiring to walk makes pedestrians naturally very conscious of their choice of routes.

People reluctantly accept large deviations from the determined main direction, and if the goal is in sight, they tend to steer directly toward it.

Whenever people walk, they prefer direct routes and short-cuts. Only very great obstacles, like dangerous traffic, extensive barriers, and so on, seem to be able to interrupt this pattern.

Just how pronounced the wish is to follow the shortest route is illustrated by a number of observations.

In a survey of a Copenhagen square (see page 140) pedestrians were found to cross the square on the diagonal, even though this meant that they had to traverse a sunken area in the middle of the square using two short sets of stairs. At the Campo in Siena (see page 42), a comparable pattern has been observed, even though this means that over a stretch of 135 meters (400 ft.) the pedestrians must first walk 3 meters (10 ft.) down the sloping pavement and then 3 meters (10 ft.) up.

In trafficked streets the tendency is to follow the shortest route instead of the safest one. Only where automobile traffic is very heavy, where the streets are very wide, or where pedestrian crosswalks are very well placed is there effective use of crosswalks.

walking routes

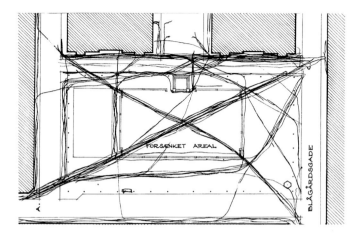

Survey of pedestrian routes on a square in Copenhagen. Nearly every-one follows the shortest routes across the square: only pedestrians pushing bicycles or baby carriages make detours around the sunken area.

The preference for right angles, commonly pursued by urban plan-ners, is not in any way shared by pedestrians.
Center left: Residential area in Holland.
Below left: walking patterns on a snowy day at the Town Hall Square in Copenhagen, Denmark.

The combination of heavy automobile traffic, barriers, and difficult street crossings results in a number of irritating detours and unreasonable restrictions on pedestrian traffic.

The situation at Kongens Nytorv, a large square in the center of Copenhagen, illustrates the problem.

Pedestrians are forced to keep to the periphery of the square and to a number of large and small islands within the space.

The pedestrian landscape of the square in the 1970's consisted of 48 islands that pedestrians could walk between, in contrast to the situation seen in old photographs, where pedestrians move across the square in a natural and leisurely fashion in all directions.

Pedestrian landscape, Kongens Nytorv, Copenhagen, 1905.

Pedestrian landscape, Kongens Nytorv, Copenhagen, 1971. Pedestrians are confined to forty-eight "pedestrian islands".

walking routes in open spaces

When walking routes are placed at the edge of an open space, pedestrians may enjoy the best of both worlds: closeness, intensity, and detail on one side; on the other side, a fine view of the entire open space. Walking routes placed in the middle of a space most often provide neither detail nor expanse of view.

walking distances and pedestrian routes	Despite the fact that it can be tiring to walk when the entire distance to a far destination is in sight, it is still more tiring and unacceptable to be forced to use routes other than the direct one when the destination is in sight. Translated into practical planning, this emphasizes the importance of careful design of pedestrian routes where the distant destination is not in view, but where the primary direction toward the destination is maintained. This should be supplemented with great respect for the direct routes over short distances, when the destination is in sight.
spaces favorable for walking	One of the most important demands on a well-functioning pedestrian system is to organize pedestrian movement to follow the shortest distance between the natural destinations within an area. When the problems of the main traffic layout are solved, however, it becomes important to place and design the individual links in the network so that the entire system becomes highly attractive.
spatial sequences	As discussed, the planning of long, straight pedestrian routes should be avoided. Winding or interrupted streets make pedestrian movement more interesting. Additionally, winding streets usually will be better than straight ones to reduce any wind disturbance.

A walking network with alternating street spaces and small squares often will have the psychological effect of making the walking distances seem shorter. The trip is subdivided naturally, in manageable stages. People will concentrate on movement from one square to the next, rather than on how long the walk actually is.

When walking routes pass between buildings the street sections should be dimensioned in proportion to the number of prospective users, so that pedestrians move in an intimate, clearly defined space and do not "drift about" in a large, half-empty area. When some sections of the route are narrow, it is also easier to create worthwhile spatial contrasts. If the streets are 3 meters (10 ft.) wide, a 20-meter-wide (65-ft.) space will, in contrast, appear to be a square.

The quality of experiencing a large space is greatly enriched when the approach occurs through a small space: when sequences and contrasts between small and large exist. If planning as a whole is to be kept in human scale, however, it is mandatory that small spaces be really small, otherwise the large spaces easily will become far too big.

When large spaces are to be crossed, it is usually most comfortable to move along the edge instead of having to traverse a broad surface or walk down the middle of the space. Movement at the edge of a space makes it possible to experience simultaneously both the large space as well as the small details of the street facade or the spatial boundary along which one walks. On one side one experiences the open field or the square, on the other side, at close quarters, the edge of a forest or a building facade. Walking along the edge of a space gives two varied experiences instead of one, and in the dark or in bad weather, being able to move along a protecting facade is, as a rule, a further advantage.

The principle of placing pedestrian routes along the edge of a large space is found in a particularly refined form in many southern European city squares, where pedestrian traffic is led through low arcades along the periphery of the square. Here people walk in pleasant, intimate spaces where they are protected from wind and weather and can enjoy a fine view of the large space from between the columns.

The opposite extreme is represented by the many paths placed in so called green belts in residential areas, which are located in the middle of the spaces, so that there are arbitrary little strips of "landscape" on each side.

Like detours, differences in level represent a very real problem for pedestrians. All large movements upward or downward require more effort, additional muscular activity, and an interruption in the walking rhythm.

As a result people tend to circumvent or avoid the problems of changing levels. In the already mentioned examples of the Copenhagen square (page 140) and the Campo in Siena, the disadvantages of changing levels are counterbalanced by the length of the detour, but in other situations where differences in level are greater or more difficult, short detours or greater risks are chosen in preference to walking up or down.

Ola Fågelmark, of the Technical University in Lund, Sweden, analyzed the pedestrian traffic moving from a bus stop on one side of a heavily trafficked street to a shopping center on the opposite side. Of the three possible choices – walking a 50-meter (160-ft.) detour via a pedestrian crosswalk, walking directly across the street, or taking a route through a pedestrian tunnel with two sets of steps – 83 percent of the pedestrians chose the detour and pedestrian crosswalk, 10 percent walked directly across the street, and only 7 percent chose the tunnel and steps. In cases in which pedestrian traffic is directed up over a high

footbridge, it is nearly always necessary to set up a fence to encourage the pedestrians to use the bridge.

The difficulties in getting multistory city centers and shopping malls to function also emphasizes pedestrians' reluctance to depart from simple horizontal traffic if they are not offered uncomplicated escalator transportation. Even then it can be difficult. There are always more customers on the ground floor of department stores than on other floors.

Comparable problems exist in multistory dwellings in which stairs often represent an important practical and psychological barrier. While one seldom gives much consideration to moving from one room to another on the same level, one often resists moving to a room one flight up or down. In the multistory dwelling, it is often a problem to ensure reasonably equal use of the various levels, and generally the lowest floor is used most frequently. Having come down, one is reluctant to go up again. Nothing says more about the stairway as a barrier than the piles of things that always lie around on the stairways in residences, waiting to be carried up or down "sometime."

Differences in level are a very real complication. In outdoor spaces there are good arguments for either completely avoiding

ramps

Stairs and steps appear to be considerably dearer to planners than to users.
Left: Garden path at the School of Landscape Architecture, Osnabrück, Germany.

A free choice between ramp and stairs in Byker, Newcastle, England

changes in level or at least designing the connecting links so that they are as easy and psychologically practicable as possible to use.

In designing manageable vertical connections, the same general rules apply as for creating acceptable horizontal links. It is important that the connection is felt to be easy and free of complications. Gradual, short ascents and descents are less difficult to move about on than long, sharp ones. A long, steep stairway is felt to be tiring, while a number of short flights of steps, interrupted by landing, comparable to a street with small squares, is psychologically more manageable. The Spanish Steps in Rome illustrate this principle elegantly.

If pedestrian traffic is led from one level to another, it is easier to start with movement downward than with movement upward. This may be a point in favor of the use of underpasses rather than bridges – at least you start by going down. It is preferable, however, if traffic problems are to be solved in this way, to lead pedestrians over or under automobile traffic in as much of a horizontal fashion as possible, for example, with gently arched bridges, or easy underpasses, so that neither the direction nor the rhythm of walking is interrupted.

ramps rather than stairs

In situations in which pedestrian traffic must be led up or down, relatively flat ramps are generally preferred to stairs.

Ramps also permit people to maneuver baby carriages and wheelchairs more easily.

The main rule for pedestrian traffic and differences in level, then, is that variations in level should be avoided whenever possible. If it becomes necessary to direct pedestrians up or down, then ramps, not stairs, should be used.

Standing

standing

Both walking and sitting activities are more comprehensive and more demanding on the physical environment than are those related to standing. Standing activities, however, will be examined thoroughly because they demonstrate very clearly some important behavioral patterns characteristic of a large number of stationary activities in public spaces. It is important, naturally, to be able to stand in public spaces, but the key word is *staying*.

stopping for a
moment

Most standing activities are of a very functional nature: stopping for a red light, stopping to look at something, stopping to fix something. These predominantly very brief stops are not influenced greatly by the physical environment. Pedestrians stop where they must do so: at the curb, along the street facade, or wherever necessary.

standing to talk to
someone

The act of standing to talk to someone belongs to this group of more or less necessary actions. Conversation situations develop when acquaintances meet and the conversation takes place on the spot on which they meet. In principle, this is a necessary action because it is impolite to avoid contact with a good acquaintance. As no one knows in advance whether the conversation will be long or short, and as none of the participants can therefore suggest moving the meeting to a suitable standing place, groups in conversation can be seen everywhere that people meet − on stairs, near shop doors, or in the middle of a space, more or less independent of time and place.

standing for a while

For stops of longer duration, another set of rules applies. Where the act evolves from the short unceremonious stop to a real staying function, when one stops to wait for something or somebody, to enjoy the surroundings, or to see what is going on, the problem of finding a good place to stand arises.

zones for staying – the edge effect

Right: Survey of the city square, Ascoli Piceno, Italy: Standing people tend to congregate around the edges of the square. People can be found standing alongside facades, under porticoes, in niches, and next to columns.

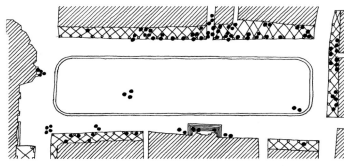

Below: Places for standing and staying in Ascoli Piceno and in a street in Amsterdam, Holland.

**zones for staying
– the edge effect**

Popular zones for staying are found along the facades in a space or in the transitional zone between one space and the next, where it is possible to view both spaces at the same time. In a study of the preferred areas for stays in Dutch recreational areas, the sociologist Derk de Jonge mentions a characteristic *edge effect* [25]. The edges of the forest, beaches, groups of trees, or clearings were the preferred zones for staying, while the open plains or beaches were not used until the edge zones were fully occupied. Comparable observations can be made in city spaces where the preferred stopping zones also are found along the borders of the spaces or at the edges of spaces within the space.

The obvious explanation for the popularity of edge zones is that placement at the edge of a space provides the best opportunities for surveying it. A supplementary explanation is discussed by Edward T. Hall in the book *The Hidden Dimension* [23], which describes how placement at the edge of a forest or close to a facade helps the individual or group to keep its distance from others.

At the edge of the forest or near the facade, one is less exposed than if one is out in the middle of a space. One is not in the way of anyone or anything. One can see, but not be seen too much, and the personal territory is reduced to a semicircle in front of the individual. When one's back is protected, others can approach only frontally, making it easy to keep watch and to react, for example, by means of a forbidding facial expression in the event of undesired invasion of personal territory.

149

if the edge works, so does the space

activities grow from the edge toward the middle

The edge zone offers a number of obvious practical and psychological advantages as a place to linger. Additionally, the area along the facade is the obvious outdoor staying area for the residents and functions of the surrounding buildings. It is relatively easy to move a function out of the house to the zone along the facade. The most natural place to linger is the doorstep, from which it is possible to go farther out into the space or to remain standing. Both physically and psychologically it is easier to remain standing than to move out into the space. One always can move farther out later on, if desired.

It can thus be concluded that events grow from inward, from the edge toward the middle of public spaces. Children congregate around the front door for a while, until they start a group game and take over the entire space. Other age groups also prefer to begin at their front doors or along the facades, from which they can go out into the space or into the house again, or merely remain.

In his book *A Pattern Language* [3], Christopher Alexander summarizes the experiences regarding the edge effect and edge zones in public spaces: "If the edge fails, then the space never becomes lively."

zones for staying –
half shade

The dappled background at the edge of the forest, under over-hanging treetops, offers another quality desirable for stationary activities – the opportunity to be partly hidden in half shade while at the same time having a fine view of the space.

Colonnades, awnings, and sunshades along the facades in city spaces provide comparably attractive possibilities for people to linger and to observe while remaining unobserved. For residences, niches in the facades, recessed entrances, porches, verandas, and plantings in the front yards serve the same purpose. Protection is provided, but there is still a good view.

standing places
– supports

Facing page: If the edge works, so does the space. Residential street, Brooklyn, New York.

Below: Something to lean on or place things near. Piazza del Campo, Siena, Italy.

Within staying zones, people carefully select places to stand in recesses, on corners, in gateways, or near columns, trees, street lamps, or comparable physical supports, which define resting places on the small scale.

The bollards that are found in many southern European city squares function widely as such well-defined supports for longer stays. These are used to stand against, to stand near, to play around, and to put things next to. In the Campo in Siena, nearly all standing activities are centered around the bollards, which are placed just at the border of the square's two zones.

good cities for staying out in have irregular facades

supports
– indoors and
outdoors

A comparable use of supports in public spaces or unfamiliar surroundings is observed in restaurants and hotel lobbies or in the first stages of a party during which guests place themselves along the walls or near furniture.

Similar observations can be made in the introductory stages of play situations, in which children often stay near furniture or various toys.

Conversely, in parks and open grass areas near residences, people often find it difficult to go out and sit on the grass if there is "nothing to sit next to."

good cities for staying
out in have irregular
facades

In summary it can be said that the design of details plays an important role in developing staying possibilities in public spaces.

If spaces are desolate and empty – without benches, columns, plants, trees, and so forth – and if the facades lack interesting details – niches, holes, gateways, stairs, and so on – it can be very difficult to find places to stop.

Or said in another way: Good cities for staying out in have irregular facades and a variety of supports in their outdoor spaces.

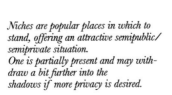

Niches are popular places in which to stand, offering an attractive semipublic/ semiprivate situation.
One is partially present and may with- draw a bit further into the shadows if more privacy is desired.

154

Sitting

well-functioning city
areas offer many
opportunities for
sitting

It is of particular importance to emphasize what good sitting arrangements mean in all types of public spaces in cities and residential areas.

Only when opportunities for sitting exist can there be stays of any duration. If these opportunities are few or bad, people just walk on by. This means not only that stays in public are brief, but also that many attractive and worthwhile outdoor activities are precluded.

The existence of good opportunities for sitting paves the way for the numerous activities that are the prime attractions in public spaces: eating, reading, sleeping, knitting, playing chess, sunbathing, watching people, talking, and so on.

These activities are so vital to the quality of public spaces in a city or residential area that the availability or lack of good sitting opportunities must be considered an all-important factor in evaluating the quality of the public environment in a given area.

To improve the quality of the outdoor environment in an area by simple means, it is almost always a good idea to create more and better opportunities for sitting.

good places to sit

The act of sitting makes several important general demands on the particular situation, the climate, and the space. These general demands are examined in greater detail in a later section.

Some specific demands relate to the sitting location and are largely the same as for spaces in which those activities involving standing take place.

The demands are reinforced, however, because the act of sitting is considerably more demanding than the more casual and transitory forms of stopping and standing. Sitting activities in general take place only where the external conditions are favorable, and the sitting locations are chosen far more carefully than are locations for standing.

choice of sitting places

Benches placed in the middle of open spaces look interesting on architectural drawings but are definitely less inviting than more sheltered spaces.

The most popular places to sit can be found at the edges of open spaces, where the sitter's back is protected, the view unobstructed, and the local climate most favorable.

choice of sitting places

The previously discussed edge effect can also be observed in relation to people's choices of sitting places. Places for sitting along facades and spatial boundaries are preferred to sitting areas in the middle of a space, and as in standing, people tend to seek support from the details of the physical environment. Sitting places in niches, at the ends of benches, or at other well-defined spots and sitting places where one's back is protected are preferred to less precisely defined places.

Several studies illustrate these tendencies more specifically.

In his study "Seating Preferences in Restaurants and Cafés," the sociologist Derk de Jonge found that restaurant seats with the backs or sides to the wall and with a good view of the general situation were preferred to other seating [26]. Window seats in particular, from which the outdoor as well as the indoor space is visible, were preferred. Those who seat people in restaurants will confirm that many guests, both singly and in groups, refuse categorically to accept a table in the middle of the room if there is any possibility at all of getting a seat along a wall.

placement of seating

Seating placement requires careful planning. There are examples everywhere of how seating is set up at random and with very little thought. It is not unusual to see ingenious bench arrangements "floating" freely in public spaces. Whether this is done because of conscious architectonic principles that disregard elementary psychological considerations or as a result of "fear of the empty space" on the design drawings, the result is frequently that these spaces, overfilled with freestanding "furniture," may look as if they have abundant opportunities for sitting but in reality offer only very poor seating.

Placement of seating must be guided by a thorough analysis of the spatial and functional qualities of the location. Each bench or seating area should preferably have an individual local quality and should be placed where there is, for example, a small

157

primary seating

*Well-designed cities offer good sitting opportunities placed carefully in the most favorable spots.
(Aberdeen, Scotland.)*

*Good places to sit and rest are very definitely a question of good benches – and inviting ones. Not any bench will do.
(Benches in Jönköbing, Sweden, and in Los Angeles.)*

space within the space, a niche, a corner, a place that offers intimacy and security and, as a rule, a good microclimate as well.

orientation and view

Orientation and view play an important role in the choice of a place to sit.

When people choose to sit in a public environment, it is almost always to enjoy the advantages the place offers – the particular place, space, weather, view of whatever is going on, and preferably all at once.

It has already been mentioned that the opportunity to see events in the area is a dominant factor in choice of sitting place, but other factors, such as sun and wind direction, are involved also. Well-protected places to sit, with an unobstructed view of the surrounding activities, are always more popular than the places offering fewer advantages and more disadvantages.

type of seating

A third and more prosaic set of demands on places to sit concerns the type of seating.

Demands vary for different groups of people. Children and young people often place only modest demands on the type of seat and in many situations accept sitting almost anywhere: on the floor, on the street, on stairs, on the edge of fountains, and on flower pots. For these groups the general situation plays a more important part than the seat does.

Other groups of people place greater demands on the type of seat.

For many people a proper seat – bench or chair – is an essential requirement for being able to sit. For many old people, in particular, the comfort and practicality of the seat is important. A seat needs to be easy to sit down on and get up from, as well as comfortable to remain on for an extended period of time.

primary seating

A well-equipped public space therefore should offer many different opportunities for sitting in order to give all user groups inspiration and opportunity to stay. *Primary seating* – benches and chairs – should be provided partly for the more demanding categories of users, partly for the situations where the need for seating is limited. When there is enough room, the best placed and most comfortable seating is preferred. The general demand is that an adequate amount of primary seating should be provided and placed in carefully chosen, strategically correct locations – those places that offer users as many advantages as possible.

secondary seating

sitting landscapes

Stairs, facade details, and all kinds of urban furniture should as a rule provide a wide range of supplementary, secondary sitting opportunities.
Right: Sitting landscapes at the Sydney Opera House and at Pioneer Courthouse Square, Portland, USA.

secondary seating

In addition to primary seating, many opportunities for supplementary, *secondary seating* in the form of stairways, pedestals, steps, low walls, boxes, and so on, are needed for times when the demand for seating is particularly great. Steps are especially popular, because they serve as good lookout points as well.

A spatial design based on an interplay between a relatively limited number of primary seating opportunities and a large number of secondary places to sit also has the advantage of appearing to function reasonably well in periods when there is only a modest number of users.

Conversely, many empty benches and chairs, such as are found during off-season periods at sidewalk cafés and resort hotels, easily can give the depressing impression that the place has been rejected and abandoned.

161

"sitting landscapes"
– multipurpose city
furnishings

A special kind of secondary seating can be provided in the form of *"sitting landscapes"* – multipurpose elements in city spaces such as a grand stairway arrangement that doubles as a lookout point, a monument, a fountain with a wide, terraced base, or any large spatial element designed to serve more than one purpose at the same time.

The design of multipurpose city furnishings and facade details with varied possibilities for use is a principle that can be generally recommended, because it results in more interesting city elements and permits a greater diversity in the use of the city space.

Venice is noteworthy in this regard because all city furnishings – street lamps, flagpoles, statues, and so forth, as well as many of the buildings – are designed so that it is also possible to sit on them. The entire city is sittable.

benches for resting
every 100 meters
(300 ft.)

Besides the primary and secondary opportunities for sitting, which are more or less designated for recreational sitting activities, there is also a considerable need for benches to rest on, placed at regular intervals throughout the city. In discussions with residents of various sections of Copenhagen, the lack of places where old people can sit is one of the most frequently named problems. A good rule of thumb for a good city or residential environment is that suitable places to sit should be located at regular intervals, for example, every 100 meters (330 ft.).

A bench for resting every 100 meters (300 feet). Please!

Seeing, Hearing, and Talking

seeing – a question of distance

The opportunities for seeing other people are, as has been discussed, a question of distance between observer and object. If the streets are too wide and the spaces too big, the opportunity of being able to view, from one place, the space and the events going on is more or less lost. This overview and the sensory command of a large, diverse scene is highly valued in most situations. It is therefore often appropriate to dimension large public spaces so that the borders of the space correspond to the limits of the social field of vision. In this way there is room for a wide range of activities, all within full view of everyone using the space.

To achieve this it is wise to work with combinations of several social fields of vision at a time, for example, the maximum distance for seeing events (70 to 100 meters – 230 to 330 ft.) combined with the maximum distance for seeing facial expressions (20 to 25 meters – 65 to 80 ft.).

In his book *Site Planning* [37], Kevin Lynch gives spatial dimensions of around 25 meters (82 ft.) as immediately comfortable and well dimensioned in a social context. He also points out that spatial dimensions greater than 110 meters (360 ft.) are seldom found in good city spaces.

It is hardly a coincidence that the length and width of most Southern European medieval city squares are near to or below these two figures.

seeing – a question of field of vision and overview

Possibilities for seeing are also a question of overview and field of vision, of unobstructed sight lines. In theaters and movie theaters, audience seating often is designed in an amphitheater form, and in lecture halls the speaker's platform or the audience is elevated so that everyone can see.

Comparable principles can be used to advantage in city spaces, to give every person optimal conditions for seeing what is going on in the space.

seeing

Viewers of all ages should be able to see what is happening. Left: Child-size window in a kindergarten and a window for young passengers on a ferry.

Seeing is a matter of good views and unobstructed lines of vision. Below: Cathedral Square, Strasbourg, France Facing page: Madrid, Spain

In this regard medieval city squares offer many examples of appropriate design. Italian city squares very commonly have pedestrian areas that are raised two or three steps in relation to the motor traffic areas.

In the Campo in Siena (see page 42), the principle is used in its most refined form. The entire square is built like a grandstand – a shell with places for standing and sitting at the top, along the facades at the shell's periphery.

This arrangement provides optimal possibilities for standing and sitting in the edge zones, at bollards, and in sidewalk cafés. The places for standing are well defined, people's backs are protected, and there is an outstanding view over the entire urban arena.

seeing – a question of light

Possibilities for seeing are also a question of adequate light on the objects to be seen. To the extent that public spaces are to function in periods of darkness, lighting is crucial.

Lighting of the socially relevant subjects is particularly important: lighting of people and faces. Out of consideration for both the general feeling of enjoyment and security and the possibilities for seeing people and events, it is desirable that lighting of pedestrian areas be ample and well directed at all times.

Better lighting does not necessarily mean brighter light.

Better lighting means an adequately bright level of lighting directed or reflected toward the vertical surfaces – faces, walls, street signs, mailboxes, and so forth – in contrast to the lighting of traffic streets. Better light also means warm and friendly light.

hearing and talking

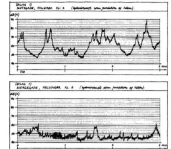

*Conversation in a pedestrian city
(Venice) and in a vehicular road
(Copenhagen).*

*Noise readings from a vehicular road
and a pedestrian street. The noise level
on the pedestrian street is even and
rather low: 50 decibels.*

hearing

Every time a street with automobile traffic is converted to a pedestrian street, there are renewed opportunities for hearing other people. The noise of cars is replaced by the sound of steps, voices, running water, and so forth. It is again possible to have a conversation, to hear music, people talking, children playing. In these traffic-free streets and in old pedestrian cities, it is possible to study how valuable and important the opportunity for hearing is for the general ambience and for physical and psychological well-being.

noise versus conversations

When background noise exceeds approximately 60 decibels, which is usually the case in streets with mixed traffic, it is nearly impossible to have ordinary conversations. It is therefore relatively rare to see people in conversation on busy streets, and where conversations do take place, they do so with great difficulty. Communication becomes an exchange of short, preplanned sentences shouted between participants during lulls in the traffic. To have a conversation under these conditions, people must stand alone close together and speak at distances of as little as 5 to 15 centimeters (2 to 6 in.). Adults and children can speak to each other under these conditions only when the adult bends down to the child, a circumstance that in effect means that adult-child communication all but disappears when the noise level is too high. Children cannot ask about what they see, and they cannot be answered. Only when background noise is less than 60 decibels is it possible to hold a conversation, and the level must be reduced to 45 to 50 decibels for people to hear most of the other loud and soft sounds of voices, footsteps, songs, and so on, which are part of the complete social situation [1],

hearing people and music

The greatest impression on the new arrival standing at the stairway outside the train station in Venice is not the canals, houses, people, and absence of cars, but the sound of people. It is seldom possible to hear people in other European cities.

For persons walking through sections of the Copenhagen pedestrian street network, it is comparable experiences, and especially the ability to hear music, song, shouts, and speech, that contribute to making the walk interesting and enriching. Spontaneous street music in Copenhagen has had a remarkable revival following the introduction of pedestrian streets, and today street music is one of the city's greatest attractions. The annual Jazz Festival staged in the streets and squares of the city is by now one of the cultural highlights. Before the introduction of traffic-free spaces, it was usually not possible to hear anything at all.

talking	Opportunities for talking with other people greatly influence the quality of outdoor spaces. It is possible to distinguish three different categories of outdoor conversation, each making different demands on the environment: conversations with people one accompanies, conversations with acquaintances one meets, and finally, possible conversations with strangers.
talking with people one accompanies	The prerequisites for talking with companions – friends, family, and so on – are described in the preceding paragraphs. These conversations take place while walking, standing, or sitting. There are ostensibly no special requirements regarding place or situation besides the requirement of an adequately low noise level. Most conversations in public spaces fall into this category of husband and wife, mother and child, friend and friend, talking together while they walk in the city.
talking with acquaintances one meets	Another category of conversation arises when friends and acquaintances meet. These conversations take place without any great dependence on place and situation. People stop to talk where they meet. Conversations with friends and neighbors who "pass by" belong to this category. The longer the outdoor stays in an area last, the greater are the chances that friends and neighbors meet and talk. The contact can be of all varieties from the brief greeting to an exchange of a few remarks to a long, satisfying chat. Conversations develop where the meeting takes place – across the hedge, at the garden gate, at the front door. Whether or not conditions make it possible to linger outside the dwelling for any length of time appears to be more of a determining factor in conversation development than the place.
talking with strangers	A third and relatively rare category of conversation in public spaces consists of conversations between people who do not already know one another. These conversations can start when the participants are at ease, in particular when they are occupied with the same thing, such as standing or sitting side by side, or while engaging in the same activity together. Concerning conversations between people who know each other and people who do not, Erving Goffmann writes in *Behavior in Public Places* [22]: One might say, as a general rule, that acquainted persons in a social situation require a reason not to enter into a face engagement with each other, while unacquainted persons require a reason to do so.

168

Something to talk about.
(From the preparations for the
annual carnival in Copenha-
gen.)

something to talk
about

Common activities and experiences as well as unexpected or
unusual events serve to initiate and generate conversation. In
The Social Life of Small Urban Spaces [51], William H. Whyte uses
the term *triangulation* to describe this phenomenon, as, for example in the interrelationship between street performers and
audience. Spectators A and B exchange smiles or begin to talk
while enjoying the skills and talents of the street entertainer, C.
A triangle is formed, and a tiny but very enjoyable process
has begun to develop.

conversation
landscapes

The design of places for sitting and standing, and their relative
location, can have a direct influence on the opportunities for
conversation. In *The Hidden Dimension* [23], Edward T. Hall
discusses a number of studies and observations concerning bench
arrangements and conversation possibilities. Bench placement,
as exemplified by waiting rooms in train stations, in
which benches are arranged back to back or with a great deal of
space in between, inhibits conversations or makes them impos-

169

sible. Conversely, chairs placed close together around a table, such as in sidewalk cafés, help conversations start.

Good conversation landscapes can be found in traditional European train compartments. In contrast, seating arrangements in airplanes and in many new trains and buses discourage conversations. Here the passengers sit behind one another and see only the backs of the heads of their fellow passengers. The risk of sitting opposite a difficult fellow traveler is removed, but most chances of starting a friendly conversation during the trip are also gone.

In planning city and residential public spaces, designers should try to place benches that allow for more choice of action than the previously mentioned straightforward "back to back" or "face to face" arrangements. For example, curved benches or benches placed at an angle to one another often will permit a valuable choice of action. When sitting at an angle to one another it is a bit easier to start a conversation if there is mutual interest in doing so, and if conversation is not wanted, it is also easier to free oneself from an undesired situation.

Such conversation landscapes have been a guiding principle for architect Ralph Erskine, who has used them widely in his residential building projects. Almost all benches in his public spaces are arranged two and two, placed at right angles around a table, which gives additional possibilities for taking work and refreshments out into the public spaces. Thus the sitting area facilitates a number of functions beyond merely sitting.

It is easier to engage in conversation when benches are placed at an angle.
Right: "Conversation landscape." (Architect Ralph Erskine.)

A Pleasant Place in Every Respect

a pleasant place in
every respect

A characteristic common to all optional, recreational, and social activities is that they take place only when the external conditions for stopping and moving about are good, when a maximum number of advantages and a minimum of disadvantages are offered physically, psychologically, and socially, and when it is in every respect pleasant to be in the environment.

a question of
protection

The pleasantness of a place is partly contingent on protection from danger and physical harm, primarily protection from insecurity due to fear of criminality and vehicular traffic.

protection from crime

Where crime is a general problem, protection is a dominant consideration, a factor that has a prominent place in Jane Jacobs's treatment of planning problems in large U.S. cities [24]. Jacobs has examined the relationship between activity level and degree of safety on a street. If there are many people on a street, there is considerable mutual protection, and if it is lively, many people survey the street from their windows because it is meaningful and entertaining to keep up with events.

The effect this natural "street watching" can have on safety is illustrated by accident statistics from the pedestrian city of Venice, where there are practically no drownings in its numerous canals. Due to the slow traffic and resulting high activity level on and along the canals, there is always someone among the passersby or among those looking out of their windows who will be watching when an accident occurs and thus can intervene.

In *Defensible Space* [40] Oscar Newman presents comprehensive documentation that further emphasizes the importance of street activities, of resting opportunities immediately in front of dwellings, and of good opportunities for looking out at public spaces, in reducing crime and vandalism in a given area.

protection from vehicular traffic

The ever-present fear of vehicular traffic is one of the most pressing problems in traffic-dominated cities.

Below: The price of fear – restriction of children under six on vehicular streets in Australia. Hardly any children are allowed to roam freely on the sidewalks of trafficked streets, while on pedestrian streets almost no children are constrained to walk hand in hand with their parents.

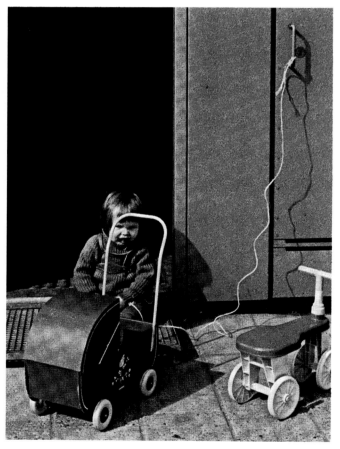

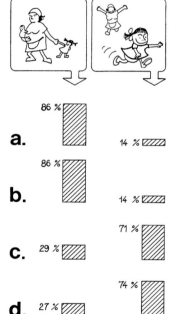

a. 86 % — 14 %

b. 86 % — 14 %

c. 29 % — 71 %

d. 27 % — 74 %

a: Trafficked street 1, Melbourne.
b: Trafficked street 2, Melbourne.
c: Pedestrian street, Melbourne.
d: Pedestrian street, Sydney.

The natural surveillance of public areas is one factor in this context. Equally important are the natural interest and feeling of responsibility created when residents themselves have outdoor areas they can use comfortably and when access roads and open areas are clearly connected to the individual residences or groups of residences in the form of precisely defined common areas, rather than as undefined and underused tracts of no-man's-land.

protection from
vehicular traffic

Another significant safety requirement is protection from vehicular traffic. If this demand is not adequately satisfied, the result is extensive restriction of both the scope and character of outdoor activities. Children must walk hand in hand with adults. Old people are afraid to cross the street. Even on the sidewalk it is not possible to feel completely safe.

Planners must take into consideration that it is the feeling of risk and uncertainty rather than actual statistical risk that plays the decisive role in a given situation. This implies that it is necessary to work carefully with both the actual traffic safety and the feeling of security with regard to traffic.

An investigation of Australian vehicular and pedestrian streets illustrates how secure people feel in these two types of street and the safety precautions pedestrians are forced to take in the vehicular streets in particular. Of all children up to six years of age who were on the sidewalks on ordinary vehicular streets, 86 percent walked hand in hand with an adult. On pedestrian streets the figure was almost reversed, and 75 percent of the children were allowed to run around freely.

Although a traffic-free situation, such as is found in pedestrian areas, is by far the best solution with regard to safety and the feeling of security, it should be noted that the Dutch *Woonerf* principles of slow vehicular traffic in predominantly pedestrian and bicycle streets represent a remarkable improvement compared with the situation commonly found in city streets.

protection from
unpleasant weather

Creating a pleasant place is a question of protection from unpleasant weather as well. Types of undesirable weather conditions vary considerably from area to area and country to country. Each region has its own climatic conditions and cultural patterns, which must be the basis for the solutions in each individual case. Protection from sun and heat plays an important part in southern Europe during the summer months, while the problems of northern Europe are quite different.

173

climatic problems

By far the greatest problem in outdoor spaces is wind. When the wind is blowing, it is difficult to keep one's balance, to keep warm, and to protect oneself.

Rain without wind is not a major problem. A canopy or umbrella provides ample protection. (Venice.)

It is reasonably easy to protect oneself against the cold as long as it is not accompanied by wind or downpour. A sunny, clear day with no wind is generally considered a lovely day, regardless of temperature.
Above: A winter day with frost, sun, and calm weather on a square in Copenhagen. All sunlit benches are in demand.

The following discussion emphasizes the situation in northern Europe, and Scandinavia in particular, where climatic protection, not surprisingly, has been the object of particularly comprehensive treatment.

The problems in Canada and large parts of the United States and Australia, however, are not very different from the problems in northern and middle Europe.

climate and outdoor activity patterns

In Scandinavia the correlation between climate and the extent and character of activities is illustrated by a survey of pedestrian street activities in Copenhagen in the period from January to July [18]. During this period, as winter changed to summer, the number of pedestrians doubled and number of people standing tripled, as a result of more frequent and lengthy stops. At the same time, changes in the character of activities related to standing were observed, as stops to eat, drink, and sightsee increased in number. Street performances, exhibitions, and other events that were practically nonexistent during the winter played a large part in the total activity pattern in the warmest months. Finally, sitting activities, which were at an absolute zero in the coldest period, soared when the temperature around the individual benches reached a temperature above 10°C (50°F).

In summary, in January (at +2°C/36°F) the activity distribution of people was approximately 30 percent standing and 70 percent moving, while in July (at +20°C/68°F) the majority of activities − 55 percent − were standing and sitting activities. The pedestrian streets had changed subtly into streets predominantly used for standing and sitting.

A study of comfort and climatic conditions in San Francisco carried out by Peter Bosselmann [5] reveals an interesting similarity between the situations in San Francisco and Scandinavia:

Most of the time, people outdoors require direct sunshine and protection from the wind to be comfortable. On all but the warmest days, parks and plazas that are windswept or in shadow are virtually deserted, while those that offer sunlight and protection from the wind are heavily used.

In his examination of the social life of small urban spaces in New York, William H. Whyte [51] also emphasizes the importance of protection against negative climatic conditions in order to assure acceptable conditions for the outdoor activities.

175

climate protection and site planning

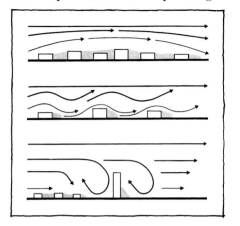

A site plan can greatly improve or worsen the local climate. Wind tends to bypass low, densely built areas, but it is caught, directed downward, and intensified by tall freestanding buildings.

In the low, moderately built-up area, the annual number of acceptable hours for outdoor stays can easily be twice as high as that for the surrounding open land.

The climate around high spread-out buildings will generally be significantly more severe than that in surrounding open land. High-rise housing area, southern Sweden: Windbreaks must be placed around sandboxes to prevent the sand — and the children — from blowing out.

the ability to function year-round requires protection from climatic conditions

During recent years recognition of the close connection between climate, comfort, and activity patterns has spread quickly within the commercial sector, where shopping centers, large stores, hotel lobbies, railway stations, and air terminals are climate-controlled as a matter of course.

A comparable development has been seen in the residential sector, where in a few places there has been an effort to make it possible for public spaces in residential projects to be used year-round.

Interest in creating improved conditions in other types of urban spaces has also increased in recent years; publications and conferences initiated by the Canadian/Scandinavian organization "Livable Winter Cities" are an example [42]. Other good examples, however, are still extremely rare. It is far more the norm to see adverse climatic conditions resulting from thoughtless planning.

protection from climatic conditions – in city and site planning

Many problems can be avoided if careful work is done at the city and site planning level to reduce the effects of the most annoying climatic factors.

In Scandinavia the main problem has always been the wind and the accompanying cooling, making climate-conscious city and site planning vitally important.

In Denmark traditional buildings in the old towns are low, attached buildings, placed along narrow streets, with small courtyards behind the build-ings. When the west wind meets these low settlements, most of the wind is conducted over them. At the same time, sunshine is captured and held, because the buildings are low and the outdoor spaces small and carefully oriented toward the sun. In these towns the local climate is considerably better than in the surrounding open countryside, and the annual number of hours that one can comfortably remain outdoors is much greater. In terms of climate, these towns are "moved" many hundred kilometers south because of appropriate design.

In new building projects, for example, in spread-out single-family housing areas and particularly around multistory residential buildings, the local climate is far poorer. The climate in the outdoor areas in front of many multistory buildings is much worse than in the surrounding open land. This is especially true for the high-rise buildings, which catch the strong winds 20, 30, and 40 meters above ground and direct them downward toward the surface, where they chill everything and everybody and blow sand out of the sandboxes.

177

If the outdoor climate and the opportunities for outdoor stays in a traditional Danish small town are compared with the possibilities around new multistory buildings, it is not unusual to find that the "summer" (or outdoor season) in the low, attached building project is two months longer than it is near the multistory buildings [44], and that the low city can offer up to twice as many acceptable outdoor hours annually as the tall one can.

In many American and Canadian cities, almost arctic conditions have been created by thoughtless placement and detailing of tall buildings. In *Sun, Wind and Comfort* [5], Peter Bosselmann, apart from pointing to the undesirable shadow effect, gives eight examples of climate deterioration due to wind around free-standing high-rise buildings, among them the channel effect, the corner effect, and the gap effect. William H. Whyte [51], writing about conditions in New York, points to the consequences:

> It is now well established that very tall free-standing towers can generate tremendous drafts down their sides. This has in no way inhibited the construction of such towers, with the result, predictably, that some spaces are frequently uninhabitable.

protection from
climate conditions
– in detail planning

Both city and site planning can, as mentioned, improve or worsen the local climate and thereby create a better or poorer general situation. Crucial to outdoor comfort and opportunities for remaining outdoors is, however, the microclimate in these areas and on the pedestrian routes themselves – the climate on and around the bench where one wants to sit or the climate on the sidewalk where one wants to walk.

It is thus important for planners to place walking routes and outdoor resting areas optimally in relation to the microclimatic factors of each specific place. Moreover, efforts should be made on the small scale to help the situation by providing windbreaks, trees and hedges, and covered areas precisely where they are most needed.

experiencing the
weather

The relationship between city activities and the weather is not satisfactorily provided for through one-sided protection from unpleasant climatic conditions. It is fine to be protected from the worst climatic effects, but it is also desirable to have the opportunity to experience good and bad weather, seasonal changes, and so forth, particularly when it is possible for a person to decide for himself when he wishes to do so. In any case it is nice to experience the pleasant weather when it is there.

*It will often be possible –
with modest means – to create a
pleasant climate just at the spot
where it is most needed.*

enjoying the positive
aspects of the weather

"Mad dogs and Englishmen go out in the midday sun." The
English have, quite understandably, a special love affair with
the sun. The same is true of Scandinavians. The same love of
sunshine can be found in many other parts of the world – at any
rate in the spring and autumn.

The wish to be able to enjoy the positive aspects of the weather
makes it important to handle the problems of climatic protection
sensitively.

In England and Scandinavia, the dark winter and following
short and lush summer have created a special relationship
between the inhabitants, the sun, and the greenery. If it is
possible to enjoy the sun and vegetation only for a brief period,
the urge to do so is very great.

Sun worshipping is extremely widespread in the early spring
months. When the sun is shining, young and old sunbathe in
large numbers. The wish to be in the sunshine is reflected in the
choice of pedestrian routes and in the placement of people in a
space; northern Europeans automatically choose a place in the

179

sun, even at temperatures at which Italians, for example, would have sought the shade long ago.

With regard to trees and plants, a comparable devotion and appreciation can be noted in northern European countries. When trees stand leafless half the year, the pleasure is so much greater when they have leaves, and people particularly appreciate following the change of seasons in flowers, bushes, and trees. In those countries with long winters and short, lush summers, gardens and living in close contact with the earth play a far greater role than is the case in middle and southern Europe.

In the town planning in these countries, greenery has a prominent role as well. The English square is, like most Scandinavian squares, laid out with trees, bushes, lawns, and flower arrangements, in contrast to the southern European squares, which frequently are laid out without plants.

conclusion
– good protection
against bad weather,
good access to good
weather

The northern European climate and the special cultural characteristics associated with it make it important in that part of the world to work simultaneously with good climatic protection for bad weather conditions, and with assuring good access to sunshine and positive climatic factors when the weather is good. Comparable meticulous appraisal and detailing must be implemented in other parts of the world, beginning with the regional climatic conditions and cultural patterns. This is seldom an easy task, but it is always an important one, because in nearly all instances the quality of a place is closely associated with the climatic conditions, for better or worse.

a pleasant place to be – a question of aesthetic quality	The experiencing of attractions in a given space is also a question of the design of the space, of the quality of the experiences offered by the physical environment – whether or not it is a beautiful place. In earlier centuries work with the visual aspects of cities and urban spaces has been the subject of quite extensive writings. Camillo Sitte, among others, has in his outstanding work *City Planning According to Artistic Principles*, written in 1889 [45], produced a convincing argument for the connection between the architectural quality, the experiencing of attractions, and the use of the city.
a sense of place	Gordon Cullen elaborates on the concept of "sense of place" in his book *Townscape* [10]. He points out how a characteristic visual expression contributes to giving a feeling of a sense of place and through this inspires people to be in a space.

This feeling of spatial quality characterizes many old pedestrian cities and spaces. In Venice, for example, and in many famous Italian city squares, life in the space, the climate, and the architectural quality support and complement each other to create an unforgettable total impression.

When all factors have the opportunity of working together as in these examples, a feeling of physical and psychological well-being results: the feeling that a space is a thoroughly pleasant place to be in.

lengthy stays mean lively streets

Although "come and go" activities account for more than 50 percent of the total number of activities occurring on the twelve streets surveyed (Fig. 1), stationary activities are the ones that bring life to the streets.

Graph showing the frequency and duration of all types of outdoor activity on twelve residential streets in Waterloo and Kitchener, Ontario.

Because of their duration, they account for an impressive 90 percent of all time spent on the streets (Fig. 3).

Below: Characteristic street scenes in Toronto. The houses are moderately close together and have semiprivate porches facing the street.

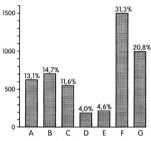

1. Number of outdoor activities.

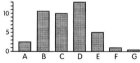

2. Average duration of activities.

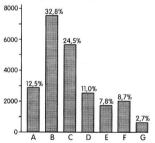

3. Total number of minutes spent on the twelve streets.

A. *Interacting*
B. *Staying*
C. *Doing something*
D. *Playing*
E. *Strolls inside area*
F. *Coming and going on foot*
G. *Coming and going by car*

Soft Edges

being able to stay
next to the buildings
– or merely able to
come and go

This final section will examine more fully how comfortable resting areas, placed on the public side of buildings and with direct connection to them, influence life between buildings. Of course it is important that conditions for walking to and from buildings are good and comfortable, but for the scope and character of life between buildings, the conditions offered for long-lasting outdoor activities play the decisive role.

A survey carried out in the summer of 1977 of the street activities in 12 streets of rowhouses and detached houses in Kitchener and Waterloo, in southern Ontario, Canada, illustrates this subject [20]. In the survey, which included 12 street sections 100 yards long each, a record was made of how many and what kinds of activities took place on porches, in front yards, and in the street itself in the course of an ordinary weekday. In addition, the duration of the individual events was recorded.

If one examines how many events took place in the 12 streets (fig. 1), one can see that the activities that involve coming and going on foot or in an automobile comprise 52 percent of the total activities.

If the average duration of the individual activities is examined (fig. 2), it can be seen that precisely these "coming and going" activities are the ones that are very brief in duration, while the various stationary activities – just resting, doing something, or play activities – are the more prolonged. (For "coming and going" activities, the time pedestrians and motorists are present in the street is taken into consideration – in other words the time it takes to walk out of the area, or the time motorists use to walk to and from their cars.) The true picture of life between buildings in the streets is revealed only when the number of activities is combined with the average duration of the individual activities (fig. 3). If the number and duration are combined, it can be seen that the numerous "coming and going" activities only account for a little over 10 percent of the total outdoor time,

183

while the stationary activities account for nearly 90 percent. This theme has been examined previously but is emphasized in this section once more; a few long-lasting activities produce exactly as much life between buildings, and just as many opportunities for meetings between neighbors, as the many short activities. This underscores the importance of providing good possibilities for stopping and resting on the public side of the houses.

The need for such spaces is emphasized further when one looks more closely at the type of activities that would disappear if only the short-term "coming and going" activities were permitted to take place.

From this starting point an examination of a series of physical factors that can be important for the scope and character of outdoor activities around various types of dwellings follows.

Some of the most important factors can be summarized in the following three main points:

- Easy access in and out.
- Good staying areas directly in front of the houses.
- Something to do, something to work with, directly in front of the houses.

multistory buildings – many coming-and-going activities, but few stationary activities

It is important that it is easy to go in and out of dwellings. If the passage between indoors and outdoors is difficult – if it is necessary, for example, to use stairs and elevators to get in and out – the number of outdoor visits drops noticeably [19, 39]. Residents in multistory buildings move about, of course, to and from their dwellings, regardless of which story they live on. This generates a comprehensive "coming and going" traffic, but many other outdoor stationary activities – especially short-term and spontaneous activities – more or less cease because it is too bothersome to come down and go out into the public areas.

The outdoor areas in the vicinity of multistory buildings further acquire a rather impersonal character in most cases, due to the special use that the residential form itself calls forth. These areas achieve a more public character. Various play possibilities are established for children, but as a rule there is not very much for adults to do. There may be fixed benches and opportunities for taking walks, but rarely more. Residents are practically cut off from using their own furniture, tools, and toys – it is simply too much trouble to carry things in and out all the time. Under these conditions outdoor activities become extremely limited, both with regard to number and character.

Poor detailing and weak indoor/outdoor connections greatly reduce the use of exterior spaces in many multistory housing areas. Generally it takes a great deal of determination and effort to overcome the built-in obstacles. (Sunday scene, Western Copenhagen.)

low buildings
– many stationary
activities, "flow" in
and out

These factors explain why outdoor activity in front of multistory buildings is so often very limited, even though a great number of people in fact live in the buildings. The residents come and go, but many of the additional activities that could take place never have a chance to develop.

Around low residential buildings with direct access to the outdoors, events in and around the dwelling have entirely different opportunities for "flowing" in and out. In contrast to the situation in multistory buildings, there is no need for people to make many decisions and preparations to go out. It is easy just to "pop out" to see what is going on, to drink a cup of coffee out on the doorstep if there is a momentary pause, and so on.

A survey of rowhouse streets with front yards in Melbourne, Australia [21], showed that 46 percent of the total outdoor stays on the public side of the houses lasted less than one minute. Throughout the day the residents moved back and forth between dwelling, front yard, and sidewalk. It was easy just to go out and correspondingly easy to go in again if there was nobody to talk to or nothing one wished to do.

Under these conditions all forms of outdoor stays are given substantially better opportunities to develop. The larger event can grow spontaneously, with a starting point in the many little visits outdoors.

being able to stay next to the buildings – or merely to come and go

Two parallel streets in Copenhagen.
Top: Hard-edged street, suitable only for brief comings and goings.
Middle and below: Soft-edged street, three times more activities take place in the course of a normal day than on the street above [19].

A gentle flow of life between public and private spaces. (Sporenburg Island, Amsterdam, Holland)

linking indoors and outdoors
– functionally and psychologically

Many details in the design of the dwelling, of the outdoor area, and of the entrance itself can be important for the use of outdoor areas. It is not enough that residential buildings are low. The plan of the dwelling must be designed so that the activities in the house can flow freely outside. This may imply, for example, that there should be doors directly from the kitchen, dining area, or living room to the outdoor areas on the public side of the house. The outdoor areas, correspondingly, must be placed in immediate juxtaposition to the rooms in the dwelling. The entrance itself should be designed so that it is as easy to pass through as possible, both functionally and psychologically.

Middle corridors, extra doors, and, particularly, changes in level between indoors and outdoors should be avoided. Indoors and outdoors as a primary rule should be on the same level. Only then is it easy for events to flow in and out.

somewhere to stay directly in front of houses

One of the reasons why relatively few activities take place in front of houses in many residential areas is undoubtedly that suitable places for outdoor stays are lacking precisely where it would be most natural to have them – at the entrance or at other places where it is equally easy to enter and exit.

places to sit at the entrance doors

The bench next to the entrance door, protected from rain and wind, with a good view of the street, is a modest but very obvious way to support life between buildings. The entrance door is used many times throughout the day, during all months of the year. If an inviting and convenient place to sit is waiting just here, experience shows that it will be used a great deal.

187

semiprivate front yards in Australia

In the older areas of such Australian cities as Melbourne, nearly all houses are provided with well-dimensioned semiprivate front yards.
The frontyard provides good opportunities for staying, and the tiny gardens await occasional gardening. These factors contribute to an unusually vivid and multifaceted street life [21].

Life between buildings can be supported further if opportunities for staying outdoors are offered in the form of a semiprivate front yard placed in the transitional zone between the dwelling and the access street.

What the presence of such front yards between dwelling and street can mean for outdoor activities and street life is illustrated by the previously mentioned study carried out in Melbourne in 1976 [21].

The traditional building form in the older sections of Australian cities is the low rowhouse with a porch and a small front yard facing the access street and a private outdoor backyard behind the house. This form of dwelling with both front yard and backyard provides a valuable freedom of choice between staying on the public side of the house and on the private side.

From the Australian study, which comprised seventeen rowhouse streets, it appeared that the front yards played a very important role in the activity in the street spaces, and that the outdoor staying activities and conversations between neighbors had particularly favorable conditions as a direct consequence of the existence of semiprivate outdoor spaces in front of dwellings.

Of the activities observed on the public side of the houses, 69 percent of all conversations, 76 percent of all passive outdoor activities (standing or sitting), and 58 percent of all active outdoor activities (people doing something – for example, gardening) took place on porches, in front yards, or over the fences between the front yards and the sidewalk.

A number of more detailed observations from the Melbourne study emphasize the special importance of front yards to opportunities for outdoor stays. Where semiprivate front yards of reasonable size and design are provided immediately in front of residences, evident opportunities for arranging effective, permanent resting areas with roofs, windbreaks, comfortable chairs, lamps, and so on exist.

Further, in these semiprivate front yards it is possible to take furniture, tools, radios, newspapers, coffee pots, and toys outdoors and leave them until the next time they are needed.

The study also illustrates the importance of design details. It is necessary for the front yard to have a size and design that makes it suitable for establishing good resting spaces. Most Melbourne front yards were very good in this respect. The houses were placed three to four meters from the sidewalk, far enough to ensure a certain measure of privacy for those sitting in front of the house, yet at the same time just close enough to the street to permit contact with events occurring in it.

The traditional residential areas of Toronto are characterized by closely spaced town houses, all of which have porches providing comfortable opportunities for sitting in front of the residences. Parking is confined to backyards.

When new houses are introduced into older areas, parking spaces and garages most often form the border to the street. In this way, streets are ruined, becoming no-man's-lands devoid of street life.

The low fences at the street side provide clear delineation of the semiprivate zones toward the street, as well as good places to stand for an easy glance up or down the street, or for a chat with neighbors. Half of all conversations in the streets studied took place with one of the participants leaning against a fence.

The importance of the detail design of the front yard becomes clear when one compares the front yards and front gardens in other areas.

In American, Canadian, Australian, and many European suburban areas, detached houses are drawn back six to eight meters from the sidewalk. Front yards are used for parking and for open lawns, with no fence toward the street. With the six- to eight-meter setback, the distance to the street is too great to permit contact between the area near the house and events happening on the street. And there is no fence to stand against when residents want to look around or to discuss something with neighbors. With regard to suburbs, it should be noted further that if the houses are too spread out, no neighbors walk by. If this is the case, the whole point of having a semiprivate front yard is moot.

semiprivate front yards
– something to do (and something to talk about)

Front yards with resting space and a small garden also have another important quality, in that there are always a number of meaningful chores to do if one wishes to stay for a while in front of the house. These tasks, for example, watering flowers, sweeping the porch, cutting the grass, painting the fence – can be both meaningful activities – sensible things to do while one is out – and explanations or excuses for being outdoors for an extended period of time.

The front yard studies in Melbourne demonstrated clearly that gardening and house maintenance had this pleasant double function. Watering flowers, sweeping the sidewalk, and so forth often took much longer than seemed necessary. If neighbors came by, work was interrupted willingly in favor of a little chat across the fence. And when someone is doing something, there is always something to talk about: "Your roses are really doing well this year."

the few square feet next to the house versus the large areas farther away

The study of rowhouse areas with semiprivate front yards in Canada, Australia, and Scandinavia emphasize that even very small outdoor areas placed directly in front of houses can have far greater and substantially more faceted use than larger recreational areas that are more difficult to reach. This does not mean that areas for sports, green lawns, and city parks are in any way superfluous, but it means that in all cases there should be areas and resources set aside to provide "immediate" recreational areas. The few well-designed square feet next to a dwelling will most often be more useful and more used than the large areas farther away.

soft edges
– in new residential areas

Recognizing the often very improvised and fluid character of outdoor activities and outlining relevant physical conditions naturally will be useful for planning all forms of new residential areas. Some of the most substantial arguments in favor of keeping buildings reasonably dense and reasonably low can be found here. If children are to be assured optimal opportunities for play and contact with other children and if the additional resident groups are to be assured not only good opportunities for experiences and contact but also a wide spectrum of outdoor recreational possibilities, it is important that events are allowed

191

semiprivate front yards, Galgebakken, Copenhagen

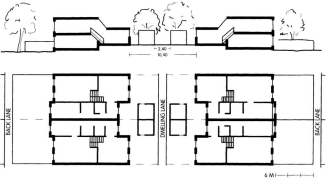

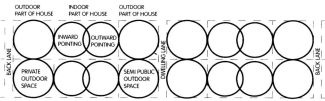

OUTDOOR PART OF HOUSE	INDOOR PART OF HOUSE	OUTDOOR PART OF HOUSE

In Galgebakken, a public housing development south of Copenhagen built in 1972-74, each dwelling is provided with a semiprivate front yard as well as a private backyard. Cars are parked at the edges of the areas; all internal traffic is on foot. (Architects A. & J. Ørum Nielsen, Storgaard and Marcussen)

Above: Site plan 1:15,000. Left: Section and plan of access lane, explanatory diagram, and photo showing the private side. Below: The semiprivate front yard facing the access lane. The useful frontyards have enabled this housing development to have 35 percent more outdoor activities than comparable new housing projects [A]. (See also page 38.)

to flow in and out of houses. And it is important that places for resting as well as opportunities for being engaged in an activity are present, directly in front of the house. In this way small, improvised events have reasonable chances for development. From the multitude of small events bigger ones may grow.

In Scandinavia, where the recreational outdoor activities are accorded a special importance because of the short summer, interest in dense-low dwelling forms is developing, while interest in multistory residential buildings and single-family houses is on the decline. Dense-low cluster-type building projects constitute the major part of all residential building production in Denmark. Opportunities for outdoor stays on the public side of these types of residences have been considerably developed, compared to the rowhouse projects of earlier periods.

One of the best examples of this category of new residential building projects is Galgebakken, with approximately 700 rental rowhouses, built in the mid-1970s west of Copenhagen [12]. The dwellings are arranged in groups of ten to twenty families, around a 3-meter-wide (10-ft.) access lane. Between the street and the houses, 4-meter-deep (13-ft.) semiprivate front yards have been laid out. The front yards are arranged and planted by the residents themselves and have proved to be very important to the outdoor activities as well. Even though the houses all have both a private backyard and a semiprivate front yard, children play in the front yards along the access lane and most additional outdoor activities take place there. A study of the outdoor activities from 1980-81 demonstrates that the residents use the front yards twice as much as they do backyards [19] (see also page 38).

Recent public housing policy in Australia has reintroduced the concept of low houses with semiprivate front yards – a concept that has worked well for 150 years and still does. Examples illustrating the former less successful policy can be seen in the background. (Melbourne)

semiprivate front yards, Byker, Newcastle upon Tyne, England

Byker, Newcastle upon Tyne, 1969-80. (Architect Ralph Erskine) Right: A balcony, a niche by the entrance, a tiny bench, a small garden, and the neighbors "at arm's length "from the kitchen window – simple but extremely useful details.

Below: If the edge of a public space works, so does the space. Carefully designed edge zone: a small terrace, a tiny garden, a bench by the door, and a screen between neighboring units.

Correspondingly meticulous design of the transitional zone between indoors and outdoors is found in Ralph Erskine's residential building projects in Sweden and England. The bench at the entrance door, the front yard with a little terrace in front of the rowhouse, and the resting space directly in front of the stairways in multistory dwellings are important design elements that contribute to creating the high quality of these residential building projects.

soft edges
– in existing building projects

The principles that now are used widely in the construction of new residential areas naturally will be applicable to the improvement of existing buildings. In low, detached houses, good possibilities often exist for softening the edges by establishing well-designed resting areas in front of houses.

The Krocksbäck public housing project, built in the mid-1960s in Malmö, Sweden, is one of many projects being extensively renovated in the mid-1980s. Special efforts are made concerning the improvement of exterior spaces, entrances, and ground floor areas next to the buildings.
Right: Housing block before improvement.
Below: Housing block after improvement.
Below right: Entrance area and semiprivate front yard.

soft edges – in all types of settings

In many instances there are also possibilities for improving the conditions for outdoor stays next to existing multistory buildings, even though the difficult access conditions between in and out will to some extent limit the actual use of the new opportunities provided.

For example, semiprivate front yards with resting places, play areas, and flower beds can be established in front of the entrance doors to every stairway, for the residents in that particular stair section.

In many places such improvements have been carried out in quite new multistory dwelling areas, such as in the multistory building projects Krocksbäck and Rosengården built in the 1960s in Malmö, Sweden, and extensively improved in the early 1980s and onward.

In these and comparable projects, efforts have been made to differentiate the residential buildings so that the large, confusing areas are clearly divided into smaller units. This division is supported by designing three or four different categories of public spaces, which are clearly defined as belonging either to the entire building project, to some few buildings, to the individual stairway entrances, or to ground-floor apartments.

In both projects work also has been done to give the areas immediately adjacent to the houses a better defined and more intimate character, in order to improve opportunities for stopping and resting precisely where there is the greatest chance that outdoor areas will be used.

soft edges
– in all types of
settings

The design principles that support outdoor stationary activities at the residential level are applicable to a great number of other building arrangements and urban functions.

Everywhere people walk to and from city functions, or where the functions within a building can profit from opportunities to come outdoors, the establishment of good connections between indoors and outdoors combined with good resting places in front of the buildings must be a matter of course.

Such an extension of opportunities for outdoor stays exactly where everyday activities take place will almost without exception be a valuable contribution to a given function and to life between buildings in the building project, in the neighborhood, and in the city.

Bibliography

1. Abildgaard, Jørgen, and Jan Gehl. "Bystøj og byaktiviteter" (Noise and Urban Activities). *Arkitekten* (Danish) 80, no. 18. (1978): 418-28.
2. Asplund, Gunnar, et al. *Acceptera*. Stockholm: Tiden, 1931.
3. Alexander, Christopher, Sara Ishikawa, and Murray Silverstein. *A Pattern Language*. New York: Oxford University Press, 1977.
4. Appleyard, D., and Lintell, M. "The Environmental Quality of City Streets." *Journal of the American Institute of Planners*, JAIP, vol. 38, no. 2. (March 1972): 84-101.
5. Bosselmann, Peter, et al. *Sun, Wind, and Comfort: A Study of Open Spaces and Sidewalks in Four Downtown Areas*. Berkeley: University of California Press, 1984.
6. *Bostadens Grannskab*. Statens Planverk, report 24. Stockholm, 1972.
7. "Byker." *Architectural Review* 1080 (December 1981): 334-43.
8. Collymore, Peter. *The Architecture of Ralph Erskine*. London: Granada, 1982.
9. *Crime Prevention Considerations in Local Planning*. Copenhagen: Danish Crime Prevention Council, 1984.
10. Cullen, Gordon. *Townscape*. London: The Architectural Press, 1961.
11. "De Drontener Agora." *Architectural Design* 7 (1969): 358-62.
12. "Galgebakken." *Architects' Journal*, vol. 161, no. 14 (April 2, 1975): 722-23.
13. "Gårdsåkra." (Nya Esle, Eslöv). *Arkitektur* (Swedish), vol. 83, no. 7 (1983): 20-23.
14. Gehl, Ingrid. *Bo-miljø* (Living Environment-Psychological Aspects of Housing). Danish Building Research Institute, report 71. Copenhagen: Teknisk Forlag, 1971.
15. Gehl, Jan. *Attraktioner på Strøget*. Kunstakademiets Arkitektskole. Studyreport. Copenhagen, 1969.
16. Gehl, Jan. "From Downfall to Renaissance of the Life in Public Spaces." *In Fourth Annual Pedestrian Conference Proceedings*. Washington, D.C.: U.S. Government Printing Office, 1984, 219-27.
17. Gehl, Jan. "Mennesker og trafik i Helsingør" (Pedestrians and Vehicular Traffic in Elsinore). *Byplan* 21, no. 122 (1969): 132-33.
18. Gehl, Jan. "Mennesker til fods" (Pedestrians). *Arkitekten* (Danish) 70, no. 20 (1968): 429-46.
19. Gehl, Jan. "Soft Edges in Residential Streets." *Scandinavian Housing and Planning Research* 3, no. 2, May 1986: 89-102.
20. Gehl, Jan. "The Residential Street Environment." *Built Environment* 6, no. 1 (1980): 51-61.
21. Gehl, Jan, et al. *The Interface Between Public and Private Territories in Residential Areas*. A study by students of architecture at Melbourne University. Melbourne, Australia, 1977.
22. Goffman, Erving. *Behavior in Public Places: Notes on the Social Organization of Gatherings*. New York: The Free Press, 1963.
23. Hall, Edward T. *The Hidden Dimension*. New York: Doubleday, 1966.
24. Jacobs, Jane. *The Death and Life of Great American Cities*. New York: Random House, 1961.

25. Jonge, Derk de. "Applied Hodology." *Landscape* 17, no. 2 (1967-68): 10-11.
26. Jonge, Derk de. *Seating Preferences in Restaurants and Cafés*. Delft, 1968.
27. Kao, Louise. "Hvor sidder man på Kongens Nytorv?" (Sitting Preferences on Kongens Nytorv). *Arkitekten* (Danish) 70, no. 20 (1968): 445.
28. Kjærsdam, Finn. *Haveboligområdets fællesareal*. Parts 1 and 2. Part 1 published by: Den kongelige Veterinær og Landbohøjskole, Copenhagen, 1974. Part 2 by: Aalborg Universitetscenter, ISP, Aalborg, 1976.
29. Krier, Leon. "Houses, Palaces, Cities." Architectural Design Profile 54, *Architectural Design* 7/8 (1984).
30. Krier, Leon. "The Reconstruction of the European City." RIBA *Transactions* 2 (1982): 36-44.
31. Krier, Leon, et al. *Rational Architecture*. New York: Wittenbom, 1978.
32. Krier, Rob. *Urban Space*. New York: Rizzoli International, 1979.
33. Krier, Rob. "Elements of Architecture." Architectural Design Profile 49, *Architectural Design* 9/10 (1983).
34. Krier, Rob. *Urban Projects 1968-1982*. IAUS, Catalogue 5. New York: Institute for Architecture and Urban Studies, 1982.
35. Le Corbusier. *Concerning Town Planning*. New Haven: Yale University Press, 1948.
36. Lyle, John. "Tivoli Gardens." *Landscape* (Spring/Summer 1969): 5 – 22.
37. Lynch, Kevin. *Site Planning*. Cambridge, Mass.: MIT Press, 1962.
38. Lövemark, Oluf. "Med hänsyn til gångtrafik" (Concerning Pedestrian Traffic). *PLAN* (Swedish) 23, no. 2 (1968): 80-85.
39. Morville, Jeanne. *Planlægning af børns udemiljø i etageboligområder* (Planning for Children in Multistory Housing Areas). Danish Building Research Institute, report 11. Copenhagen: Teknisk Forlag, 1969.
40. Newman, Oscar. *Defensible Space*. New York: Macmillan, 1973.
41. *Planning Public Spaces Handbook*. New York: Project for Public Spaces, Inc., 1976.
42. Pressman, Norman, ed. *Reshaping Winter Cities*. Waterloo, Ontario: University of Waterloo Press, 1985.
43. "Ralph Erskine." Mats Egelius, ed. 2, Architectural Design Profile 9, *Architectural Design* 11/12 (1977).
44. Rosenfelt, Inger Skjervold. *Klima og boligområder* (Climate and Urban Design). Norwegian Institute for City and Regional Planning Research, Report 22. Oslo, 1972. "
45. Sitte, Camillo. *City Planning According to Artistic Principles*. New York: Random House, 1965.
46. "Skarpnäck." *Arkitektur* (Swedish) 4 (1985): 10-15.
47. "Solbjerg Have." *Architectural Review* 1031 (January 1983): 54-57.
48. "Sættedammen." *Architects' Journal*, vol. 161, no. 14 (April 2, 1975): 722-23.
49. "Tinggården." *International Asbestos Cement Review*, AC no. 95 (vol. 24, no. 3, 1975): 47-50.
50. "Trudeslund." *Architectural Review* 1031 (January 1983): 50-53.
51. Whyte, William H. *The Social Life of Small Urban Spaces*. Washington D.C.: Conservation Foundation, 1980.

Illustration Credits

Index

Island Press | Board of Directors